BLAMELESS

Daily Inspiration Toward Healing

BRANDY WILLIAMSON

First paperback edition May 2021
First ebook edition May 2021
ISBN 978-1-7332907-2-2

Book cover and interior design by JohnEdgar.Design
Published by Revolutionary Diamond Publishing, LLC

Author & Poet, Brandy Williamson

Brandy Williamson is a poet, educator, and a follower of
Christ who is born and raised in New York City. Her goal
in life is to educate, inspire and spread the good news of
the gospel.

Acknowledgements

I want to thank my entire family, however a special shout out to my two sisters, Emily Flowers and Kamali Williamson for always supporting and encouraging me. In addition, I also want to give a special shout out to my mother, who has been my inspiration and my strength. I would not be where I am today if it wasn't for the strength that God has given you to raise 3 girls alone. I would also like to acknowledge my best friend Epyana Smith for being my third sister and for holding me accountable to writing my own poetry book, my good friend CJ Wolfe for planting the seed on how I should construct this book, and to my church family for supporting and helping me grow more in the word of God. Last but not least, I would also like to acknowledge the Christian influencers that have inspired many of my poems, Sarah Jakes Roberts, Jerry Flowers, and Karolyn Roberts. Your teachings and sermons have helped strengthen my faith and allowed me to see the light when I was in the dark.

Thank you !

Before you dive deeper...

This book is the product of how my walk with God has helped me to become shameless and liberated from the challenges and obstacles of life. As you read, may you find your way to healing along with inspiration to take your own walk with Jesus Christ.

Ephesians 1:4
"For He **chose** us in Him **before** the creation of the world to be **holy** and **blameless** in His sight.
In love"

Day 1

Give God your **heart**
and He'll **change** your habits.
Give God your **mind**
and He'll **become** your passion.

Psalm 51:10
"Create in me a **clean heart**, O God, and renew a right spirit within
me."

Day 2

When **pain** meets us,
we break up with **joy.**
We tend to **lose** the person we were,
before we turned into the person we've **become**.
But **God** is not done with your story yet,
so, **exhale** the past
and **inhale** the present.
For **YOU** are a gift
and joy is your weapon.

Exodus 33:14
"and He said, **My presence** shall go with thee,
and I **will give you rest**"

Day 3

I dumped out all **our memories.**
I locked out my insecurities.
I placed all my **trust** in the Lord.
For it is He, who brings the light to me,
in moments of **darkness,**
in seasons of **drought,**
in days and minutes when I want to tap **out.**

Proverbs 3:5
"**Trust** in the Lord with all your heart and **lean not** on your own
understanding"

Day 4

Don't **underestimate** the power of **prayer.**
God's **delay** isn't a denial.
Continue to work and **don't forget to smile.**
God's words hold power and fills up any space.
Continue to pray and **don't forget to give grace.**
God's love for you is like no other,
let your wounds heal with God's **touch and timing;**
with no complaints, no whining.
God hears you; God sees you.
Your prayers will be **answered.**

1 John 5:14
"This is the **confidence** we have in **approaching God**: that if we ask
anything according to His will, He hears us."

Day 5

Put on your boxing gloves and let your **past** know,
they can't have you anymore.
You have been preparing to face them in the rink.
With **Jesus** in your corner,
with the **bible** as your trainer,
and the **Holy Spirit** as your coach.
In order to **defeat** an enemy, you must **first**
acknowledge the very one thing that bullies you.
Recognize what instills **fear** into your heart;
You were destined to win this fight from the very start.

Philippians 4:13
"I can do **all things** through Christ who **strengtheneth** me."

Day 6

The journey of healing has more to do with **you**
than your instagram followers.
Don't look to culture to help save you;
There are too many souls **lost** in the ways of the world.
God is **everywhere,** but not everywhere in the same way.
This is why there's power in the way that you pray.

2 Timothy 1:9
"He has saved us and called us to a holy life—not because of
anything we have done but because of His own purpose and grace.
This **grace** was given us in Christ Jesus
before the beginning of time."

Day 7

They were **distractions** sent from the devil
that knows what God has planned for you.
But the devil must have **forgotten** that even
when Eve was distracted and ate from the tree,
God told her that it was her **seed** that was going to
crush the devil's head.
God still has a plan for you.
You may not be where you want to be,
but **trusting God** and **continuing to fight** the battle
will **lead** you to where you need to be.

Genesis 3:15
"And I will put **enmity between you and the woman**,
and **between** your offspring and hers;
He will crush your head, and you will strike **His** heel."

Day 8

Not **everyone** in your circle wants you to succeed
because the only thing you both have in common
is the way that you **bleed.**
That is why God will show you
how it's **dangerous** to be naïve.

1 Corinthians 15:33
"Do not be misled: **"Bad company** corrupts good character."

Day 9

There's **no love** like Jesus
and **no comforter** warmer than the Holy Spirit.
Yet you'll **find yourself** in bed with **strangers**
for **temporary pleasures;**
opening parts of yourself you haven't yet healed from
causing **another broken spirit** to touch your wounds
all because you lost your ability to feel what's real.
Learning to choose you before choosing them
is a fundamental step when wanting to heal.

2 Corinthians 1:3
"**Praise be to the God** and Father of our Lord Jesus Christ, the Father
of compassion and the **God of all comfort.**"

Day 10

What if I told you that God is going to **turn**
what tried to **break** you into fire
to **fuel** the dreams you let die;
It was **NEVER** meant for you to be in this situation,
but it took this situation for you to **reunite** with what you
have on the inside.

Psalm 104:4
"He makes winds His messengers, flames of **fire** His servants."

Day 11

You'll wake up **one** morning not feeling
like how you felt the day **after** they broke your heart.
You'll **wake up** feeling like
you have oxygen back in your lungs
and with fresh new eyes
no longer filled with unwanted tears;
but then there will be **mornings** when the hurt returns
like an **unexpected** guest on Sundays
and you wonder,
how am I going to turn them away?
Well, you don't, **invite them** to stay.
Allow yourself to feel the hurt
while you **drown** yourself in scriptures.
Let go and let God.

Jude 1:2
"**Mercy, peace**, and **love** be yours in **abundance**."

Day 12

I **still** think about you
and **wonder** if I should hit you up for **closure,**
but then I remember that **everything
happens for a reason.**
And even in the midst of all of the **confusion,**
God would send **clarification,**
which will follow **peace** that reveals
how it wasn't all you,
it wasn't all me,
but it was all God.

John 14:27
"**Peace** I leave with you; **My peac**e I give you.
I do not give to you as the world gives.
Do not let your **hearts** be troubled and do not be afraid."

Day 13

I pray that you don't **lose** to depression, molestation,
rape, drugs, sex, or anxiety;
instead **find** the **strength** that God has given you
to defeat the devil.
You are **more than the situations and the addictions**
that tried to **break you**.
You are a warrior crowned in fortitude.
The first step to **victory** of the battle is to acknowledge
that you are more **powerful** than your opponent,
and the weapons given to you from God
are **greater** than any weapon
the enemy can try to use against you.

Isaiah 53:5
"But He was pierced for our transgressions,
He was **crushed** for our iniquities;
the punishment that brought us **peace** was on Him,
and **by His wounds we are healed**."

13

Day 14

Your **mind** is the most **essential** tool in your toolbox.
That is why it is the first place the enemy likes to **attack.**
You'll find yourself having thoughts of self-doubt and
memories of past behaviors you **repented** for,
which makes you begin to question about what **God has**
already told you to be true.
All because the devil wants you to believe the **lies,**
he told you.

Proverbs 30:5
"Every word of God is **flawless**;
He is a shield to those who take **refuge** in Him"

Day 15

The hardest part about **faith**
is that you have to **align** your heart and mind
on a **thought** that isn't yet **visible to your eyes.**
We don't see the oxygen we inhale, but we know it **exist.**
We don't physically see God,
but we can't **resist**
the **many times** God has shown up in our lives.
Just because you don't see **results** right away
doesn't mean God isn't working on His end.
Continue to pray.

Hebrews 11:1
"Now faith is **confidence** in what we **hope** for
and **assurance** about what we do not see."

Day 16

God's timing is **perfect** and
He has the **best** methods on how to rescue.
That's why we should **thank** God
we do not look like what we been through.

Psalm 62:8
"**Trust in Him at all times**, you people;
pour out your hearts to Him,
for **God is our refuge.**"

Day 17

Healing is a **marathon**, not a sprint.
You don't just wake up being whole the **next day**
because you removed yourself from a toxic situation.
You have to **detox,** turn off the phone, and television.
Change the music…
sometimes even the people you lend your ear to.
Use this time **alone** to build yourself,
to pick up the bricks,
and **repair** the building blocks
to the **path** back to God.

Jeremiah 17:14
"**Heal me**, Lord, and I will be healed; **save me** and I will be saved,
for **You are the one I praise.**"

Day 18

For 3 months straight I asked God
to **strengthen** my heart
because the **hurt** was unbearable.
If He did it for **me**, He can do it for **you**.
Just make sure you're **available.**

1 Chronicles 16:11
"Look to the Lord and His **strength;** seek His face always."

Day 19

I remember my father telling me
that if I cut him off, then I'm **cutting off my blessings,**
but what he didn't tell me
was that the **blessing** God has for me,
is for me and **NO ONE** can take away
from what God has
already **assigned** to my name.
Not him, friends, exes, or the enemy,
So, this is why you should **refrain**
from **forcing toxic relationships**
that try to **disrupt** what God had already promised you.

Jeremiah 29:11
"For I know the plans I have for you," declares the Lord,
"**plans to prosper you** and not to harm you,
plans to give you hope and a future."

Day 20

I pray that through your **journey** of healing
you'll be able to **discern** what's from God
and what's from the enemy,
because the same way that God sees you working,
so does the devil in **jealousy.**

1 John 4:1
"Dear friends, **do not believe every spirit,** but test the spirits to see
whether they are from God, because many false prophets
have gone out into the world."

Day 21

Be still like the waters
silent like the moon
and calm like the air.
Be relaxed like the birds
and at peace like the clouds
while God shifts the atmosphere
and presents himself in the crowds.

Isaiah 45:7
"I form the light and create darkness;
I bring prosperity and create disaster;
I, the Lord, do all these things."

Day 22

You may have **never** been in a healthy relationship,
may have **never** received a degree,
may have been told you **weren't** able
to have children, or be cancer free.
You may have **never** seen wealth
or written a business plan,
but when GOD STEPS INTO YOUR LIFE
He'll **show** you that He **CAN!**
**He would make happen what you never saw could
happen.**
That is why the **opposite** of faith isn't fear, it's sight.
BUT, when you **trust** in Christ, He'll make it **MORE**
than alright.

Matthew 19:26
Jesus looked at them and said, "With man this is **impossible,**
but with God **all things are possible.**"

Day 23

Relationships that are heavenly will **flow** into eternity.
Relationships from the enemy
will **disturb** your peace and serenity.

Psalm 72:7
"In his days may the **righteous** flourish
and **prosperity** abound till the moon is no more."

Day 24

I always knew of God's healing **powers**
and His **miracles,**
but it wasn't **until** I met God for **myself**
that made me become more **spiritual.**

Proverbs 8:17
"I love those who love Me, and those who **seek Me find Me.**"

Day 25

Continue to be the person **God** has called you to be,
not what **culture** wants you to be.
Continue to **follow** Christ because
He'll lead you to **victory,**
whereas the devil will only lead you to **misery.**

Philippians 1:6
"Being confident of this, that **He who began a good work in you**
will carry it on to **completion** until the day of Christ Jesus."

Day 26

There will be times when you **flashback**
to those unhealthy moments
you've **experienced** in your life
and it may make you **cry**; it may stir up
the **pain** that's built up inside.
It may make you **mad, angry, and disappointed**
all over again.
What I find that helps me is listening
to a powerful sermon,
reading my favorite **verses** from the bible,
praying, and doing what I can to call God's presence
so that **I feel whole again** and receive my blessings.

Jeremiah 29:13
"You will **seek Me and find Me**
when you seek Me with all your heart."

Day 27

Today I feel **blessed.**
Today I feel as though all the **pain** and **hurt** has finally
been put to **rest.**
Today I feel **healed, complete, whole,** and **everything**
God has **imagined** me to be.
Today I feel **free.**

Psalm 118:5
"When hard pressed, **I cried to the Lord;**
He brought me into a **spacious place**"

Day 28

Healing takes work
and the **first** step to properly heal
is to **acknowledge** what brings you pain.
Jesus had to face the enemy **face to face**
and so, you must do the same.

Ephesians 6:10-11
"**Finally**, **be strong in the Lord** and in **His mighty power**.
Put on the **full armor of God**, so that you can
take your stand against the devil's schemes".

Day 29

I've **learned** that God
will **remove** people and opportunities
to create more space for the **blessings**
that He's going to bless your life with.
Leave the settling for dusk
and **trust** God with your time
because He'll make you think
that you are **filling your cup** with **water**
just for you **to end up** at the table with **wine.**

John 2:9
"When the master of the feast tasted the **water**
now become wine, and did not know where it came from
(though the servants who had drawn the water knew),
the master of the feast called the bridegroom"

Day 30

You just **completed** a month's work of healing.
I hope that **each day** you wake up with **peace**
that surpasses your understanding
because God's **touch** will **strengthen** your heart
and **adjust your standing.**

Ephesians 3:16
"I pray that out of His glorious riches He may **strengthen you with
power** through His **Spirit** in your inner being."

Day 31

Before jumping into a decision, job, or a relationship,
seek God first in prayer.
Ask God to send you confirmation
until then remain **S T I L L.**

Matthew 6:33
"But **seek first** His kingdom and His righteousness, and **all these
things will be given to you as well.**"

Day 32

We all heard that **good things** come to those **who wait.**
No! Good things come to those **who work and worship**
anytime, anywhere, and any day.
Acknowledge all that God has done
while He works on the answer to your prayer.

Hebrews 13:15
"Through Jesus, therefore, let us **continually** offer to God a **sacrifice
of praise**—the fruit of lips that openly profess His name."

Day 33

Do not seek **happiness,**
for happiness is dependent on what is happening
in your life.
Seek **joy,** the emotion that **overwhelms**
your fears and anxiety.
It is what **trusting** in God does in every situation
no matter what's happening in society.

John 15:11
"I have told you this so that my **joy** may be in you
and that your **joy** may be **complete.**"

Day 34

There is an **assignment** attached to your name.
God is preparing you to **break generational curses**.
I **challenge** you to step into your **purpose,**
trust in God and **continue** to be determined.

Psalm 9:10

"Those who know Your name **trust in You**, for You, Lord, have never
forsaken those who seek You."

Day 35

Today I woke up with the **sun**
and with the **prayers** I prayed.
Realizing that the same way the sun resurrected
from the night,
I can **resurrect** the same.

Romans 8:11
"And if the Spirit of Him **who raised Jesus from the dead** is **living
in you**, He who raised Christ from the dead will also **give life to your
mortal bodies** because of His **Spirit who lives in you**."

Day 36

Don't let the **weight** of the world
wear you out like old tennis sneakers.
Remember, there's a **bloodline** attached to your name
that **needs** you as their leader.

Ephesians 6:10
"Finally, be strong in the Lord and in **His mighty power**."

Day 37

Your true **breakthrough** isn't going to come from **likes,**
reposts, retweets, or from the **false images** you
present to the **world**
to **hide** the fact that you're drowning.
Your **breakthrough** will come
from your **encounter with God.**
God doesn't care about **perfection**. He knows your sins.
What He cares about is you returning back to
the **image of Him.**

2 Timothy 2:15
"Do your **best to present yourself to God** as
one approved, a worker who does not need to be
ashamed and who correctly handles the word of truth."

Day 38

Over and over again we **fall** in love with the **picture**
we allow our **imagination** to paint.
Instead of growing in love with **patience**
and allowing God to be the **illustrator** of the image
He wants to create.

Ephesians 5:17
"Therefore, **do not be foolish**,
but understand what the **Lord's will** is."

Day 39

Having faith is about **"Even if"**
rather than **"What if."**
"What if" speaks worries and fears.
God tells us, "peace I leave with you;
My peace I give to you"
"Even if" means that no matter what,
you **know** that it is God's words
that you can **depend on.**

Mark 9:23
"'If you can'?" said Jesus. "**Everything is possible** for one who believes."

Day 40

There will be nights when your **anxiety** will
try to **rob** you of your sleep.
There will be mornings when **depression** will
try to creep in to **steal** your smile.
But through it all, remember
that you are **loved,**
that you are **worthy,**
and you don't have to **worry.**

1 Peter 5:7
"Cast **all** your anxiety on Him because **He cares for you**."

Day 41

Sometimes all the **confirmation** you need
to walk away and leave
is **married** to the **tension** that
exist **between** what you **already know,**
from **what you choose** to believe.

John 16:13
"But when He, **the Spirit of truth,** comes,
He will **guide you** into all the truth."

Day 42

Pick your head up,
no season is permanent.
Don't let your **current** situation
stop you from evolving.
You were **born** to conquer another day
no matter how daunting it feels in the **morning.**

Romans 8:37
"No, in all these things we are **more than conquerors**
through Him who loved us."

Day 43

Through my journey of **healing,**
I've learned that **endings** are **linked** to sendings.
God always **replaces** what tried to **replace** you,
but instead, this time the **replacement** is meant
to give **birth** to a **resilient believer**
and **before you know it**, you're no longer
in need of healing, but you're now a healer.

Jeremiah 17:14
"**Heal me, Lord**, and I will be healed; **save me** and I will be saved,
for You are the one I praise."

Day 44

I had to **learn** that not **all open doors** are from **God**
and not **all closed doors** are from the devil.
God will **close doors** in your life
because He already knows
that the person that **stepped** into your elevator
is not going to the **same** level.

Psalm 32:8
"I will **instruct you** and **teach you in the way you should go**;
I will counsel you with My **loving eye on you**."

Day 45

There are times when I sit in **silence** and think about
everything that I have been through.
Sometimes I want to **laugh,**
other times I want to grab some **tissues**
because **when I think** about God's grace,
there is no other **strength** that allowed
me to **push through.**

2 Timothy 1:7
"For the **Spirit** God gave us does not make us **timid, but gives us
power, love and self-discipline.**"

45

Day 46

You may not know it yet,
but you are part of **God's strategy.**
Even **when** your path takes a **detour,**
God will casually **lead** you back to the road
He created for you.

"Psalm 119:105"
"Your word is a **lamp** for my feet, a **light** on my path."

Day 47

I woke up today **lusting** over
the memories we made at night.
It always felt good in the **moment**
but after the sex, it **never** felt right.
You **became** a soul tie I needed to break
and there were times, I **thought** it was too late.
But God, being the way maker that He is,
came right on time to turn **my crooked path straight.**

Proverbs 3:6
"In all your **ways submit to Him**,
and He will make your **paths straight.**"

Day 48

The **hardest** part about healing is
acknowledging the hurt.
It's so much easier to **ignore** the symptoms
of trauma than putting in the **work.**

Psalm 147:3
"He heals the **brokenhearted** and binds up their wounds."

Day 49

God tells us that He will **strengthen** you,
help you, and will **uphold you** with His
righteous right hand.
Therefore, don't ever let **no** woman or man
try to **destroy** what God had told you
and what He has planned.

Isaiah 41:10
"I will strengthen you and help you; I will **uphold you**
with my righteous right hand."

Day 50

Damage people can **damage** people
the same way that **healed** people
can **heal** people.
Healed or damaged,
when we **seek** God
things will become
more peaceful.

Isaiah 26:3
"You will keep in **perfect peace**, those whose minds are steadfast,
because they **trust in You.**"

Day 51

I truly **underestimated** the **impact** of relationships
and **how much** of someone's **presence**
can shift the trajectory of **who you become.**
This is why it's **important** to keep
a strong relationship with God,
it lets the devil know that he is
not welcomed.

John 10:10
"The thief comes only to **steal and kill and destroy;** I have come that
they may have life and have it to the full."

Day 52

I don't know why I **still** creep on your
instagram page,
but as days **accumulate,**
I notice the **hurt** that once existed
has **lessen** and I'm able to
see our breakup **not as a curse,**
but as a **blessing.**

Numbers 6:24
"The Lord **bless you**, and keep you."

Day 53

I **struggle** with patience,
specifically, patience with God's **timing;**
but, I learned that when I **rushed**
and did things on **my own time,**
the **progress and the process** began to **rewind.**

Psalm 9:10
"Those who know Your name **trust in You**, for You, Lord, have **never forsaken** those who seek You."

Day 54

If there's **anything** my ex taught me,
it was to **trust the process.**
It is in the **journey**
where your **character** is built
to be **stronger** than your **mindset.**
It is in the process where seeking God
will **prevent** you from burning out.

Ecclesiastes 3:1
"There is a **time** for everything, and a season for
every activity under the heavens."

Day 55

My **hope** is that these words
really **help you** feel better
and that you'll be **able** to
feel God's **presence,**
even when you're **under** the weather.

Psalm 16:11
"You make known to me the path of life;
You will fill me with joy in Your **presence,**
with eternal **pleasures** at Your right hand."

Day 56

I had to **learn** that loving **myself**
also meant **protecting my heart.**
I was prone to **heart break** because no one taught me
the **danger** of wearing my heart on my sleeves.
This is what made it **easier** for
people to take **advantage** of me.

Proverbs 4:23
"Above all else, **guard your heart,**
for everything you do flows from it."

Day 57

The **heart** is not to be trusted.
It will tell the mind **lies**
just to **avoid** fighting with the **truth.**
Trust your instincts and be lead by the Spirit
because **feelings** from
the heart can be **twisted.**
Even the **bible** says that
the heart is deceitful above all things
and desperately wicked.

Jeremiah 17:9
"The **heart is deceitful above all things** and beyond cure.
Who can understand it?"

Day 58

As I **heal**
all I want to do
is **build** my relationship with God.
Spend time with Him,
go out on **dates** that
glorify His existence,
spend nights **talking** to Him through **prayer,**
and constantly read His text messages He
placed in the **bible.**
I realize He is the only relationship
that's **essential for my survival.**

Philippians 4:19
"**And my God** will **meet all your needs** according
to the riches of His glory in Christ Jesus."

Day 59

Remembering God's promises
is what **keeps me** from going back to my **old** ways.
I know that God's **plans** for me
is going to be **greater** than what I have **envisioned**
for **myself** and for my **family.**

2 Corinthians 7:1
"Therefore, since we have these **promises,** dear friends, **let us purify
ourselves from everything** that contaminates body and spirit,
perfecting **holiness** out of reverence for God."

Day 60

You see to the corner
while **God** sees **around** it.
Sometimes things do not go as planned,
but no need to **panic**
because God **CAN** turn
ANY situation into a situation
better than you could have imagined.

Job 28:24
"For He **views the ends of the earth**
and **sees everything** under the heavens."

Day 61

It's **important** to know God's words
because **non-believers**
will try to **downplay** God's **power.**
That is why it's important
to **read** your bible.
You'll **become** more of a **believer**
and **less** of a **doubter.**

Psalm 119:67
"Before I was afflicted, I went **astray**, but now I **obey Your word.**"

Day 62

I **remember** the days when
I **used** to thank God for you, but
now I can **only** imagine how
God was shaking His head
knowing I was **wasting**
time with you.

Isaiah 43:18
"**Forget** the former things, do not **dwell** on the past."

Day 63

The part that **hurts** most is that
I **believed** in you…
thought our love was **real and true**
and when we **broke up**
I **didn't know** how I was going to make it through;
but, God came to my **rescue.**

Revelation 21:4
"He will **wipe every tear from their eyes**. There will be no more
death' or mourning or crying or pain, for the old
order of things has passed away."

Day 64

Pastor Jerry Flowers said,
"If God was **patient** with us during our **rebellion**,
then **why** can't
we be **patient** with God **during our renewal?**"
Ever since that day I **stopped**
questioning God's timing
and instead began to **wait** for His approval.

Romans 12:12
"Be joyful in hope, **patient** in affliction, **faithful** in prayer."

Day 65

No **season** is **permanent.**
You may struggle in winter because of the **changes** you've
experienced in autumn;
but, spring and summer will bring **light into your life**
to **remind** you that you **haven't** hit rock bottom.

John 1:5
"The **light shines in the darkness,**
and the **darkness has not overcome it.**"

Day 66

I **used** to think that God
only existed
in the clouds,
until I **started** seeing
God in the **crowds.**

Jeremiah 23:24
"Who can hide in a secret place, so that I cannot
see them?" declares the Lord.
"Do not **I fill heaven and earth?**" declares the Lord."

Day 67

God tells us to **walk by faith**
and **not by sight**
because He **understands**
that if we knew
everything He was doing in our lives
we'd **ruin** the plans.

2 Corinthians 5:7
"For we **live by faith**, not by **sight**."

Day 68

We were not **meant** to be alone.
When the creator created Eve for Adam,
He saw that it was a **good** thing;
Therefore, be **patient** with your
love and let God **take care** of
everything.

Genesis 2:18
"Then the Lord God said, "It is **not good** that the man should be
alone; I will make him a **helper** fit for him."

Day 69

It's okay to **still** feel hurt and heartbroken.
Healing takes time, just **trust** the process.
I **promise** you will be fine.

Proverbs 13:12
"**Hope deferred** makes the heart sick, but a **longing fulfilled** is a tree
of life."

Day 70

In the **moment** it feels like your **heart** will remain
bruised forever,
but my love, **continue** to pray
and with each day, you will **begin to feel better.**

1 Thessalonians 5:17
"Pray continually."

Day 71

It's so **easy to lose focus** on your **calling**
and **distract yourself** with a counterfeit.
Do not **ignore the red signs,**
just to be in a relationship.

Hebrews 12:2
"Fixing our eyes on Jesus, **the pioneer and perfecter of faith.**
For the joy set before Him He endured the cross, scorning its **shame**,
and sat down at the right hand of the throne of God."

Day 72

You **will** see that you will
be so much **stronger** by the end of this season,
and how **everything** happened
the way that it did for that exact **reason.**

Ecclesiastes 3:1
"There is a **time for everything**,
and a **season** for every activity under the heavens."

Day 73

Everyone **always** preaches about
the great side of God,
but let's not **forget** that God would also
flip your life upside down.
He will let things **die,** just to show you
that you **can't** do **life** without Him by your side.

Hebrews 12:6
"…because the **Lord disciplines** the one He loves,
and He chastens everyone He accepts as His son."

Day 74

Everyone in your life is either **a lesson or a blessing;**
therefore, we should **appreciate** our blessings
and **learn** from our lessons.

Ephesians 1:3
"Praise be to the God and Father of our Lord Jesus Christ,
who has **blessed us in the heavenly realms**
with every spiritual blessing in Christ."

Day 75

I **learned** that God
doesn't **operate** in **confusion,** the enemy does.
If you are in a relationship
where you find yourself often **confused**
on where you two stand,
then most likely, God **did not approve** that person to be
your woman or your man.

Corinthians 14:33
"For God is not a God of **disorder but of peace** as in all the
congregations of the Lord's people."

Day 76

I find that I **still struggle** with letting you go entirely.
The **challenge** is managing both, a break-up and anxiety,
while at the **same** time, building with God
to **help** keep my insanity.

2 Corinthians 12:9
"But He said to me, "**My grace is sufficient for you**,
for My **power** is made **perfect in weakness.**"

Day 77

I've heard the saying, **"fake** it until you make it"
to **cope** with the **struggles** you hold in your heart;
but, this is honestly the **quickest** way to **tear you apart.**
Jesus and therapy are **healthier** starts.

Matthew 11:28
"**Come to Me**, all you who are **weary and burdened,**
and I will **give** you rest."

Day 78

You'll have days when it's **hard** to make it through.
You'll **feel** like you can't **focus** or **discern**
when God has spoken.
I find that **prayer lifts me up** when
I feel like I'm at my lowest.

Jeremiah 29:12
"Then you will **call on Me and come and pray to Me,**
and I will **listen** to you."

Day 79

Try not to **overwhelm** yourself
by keeping yourself **busy** just to **avoid** your mind.
Find a good **balance**
between being **productive** and giving **God your time.**

Proverbs 11:1
"The Lord detests dishonest scales,
but **accurate weights** find favor with Him."

Day 80

The more **time** I spent **learning** about God,
I realized I needed to flush out
anger, grief, and jealousy.
For these are the **emotions**
birthed from the **enemy.**

1 John 3:3
"All who have this **hope in Him purify themselves,**
just as He is pure."

Day 81

Your healing journey happens gradually.
First it happens in the **mind**
shifting your mentality,
then you'll see results
shifting your **reality.**

Romans 12:2
"**Do not conform** to the pattern of this world
but be transformed by the **renewing of your mind.**"

Day 82

God is the **author** of our path.
You'll see Him place **"periods"** after situations we weren't
strong enough to end on our own.
He'll place **commas,** in areas in our lives where we need
to **pause** and be **alone.**
Ultimately, He already **knows** our story,
the challenge is **walking with faith** and not with worry.

1 Peter 1:3
"Praise be to the God and Father of our Lord Jesus Christ! In His
great **mercy** He has given us new birth into a living hope
through the **resurrection of Jesus Christ** from the dead."

Day 83

I had to **learn**
that not **everyone** is how
they **make** themselves appear to be,
which is how I got **caught**
with a **counterfeit**
instead of the man God has for me.

1 John 3:8
"The one who does what is **sinful** is of the devil,
because the devil has been **sinning** from the beginning."

Day 84

Give yourself **time** to **heal**.
Don't throw yourself in the ocean because you **heard** the saying,
"There's plenty of fish in the sea."
Remember, sharks exist too
and are **attracted** to the blood that you bleed.

Psalm 90:12
"**Teach us** to number our days, that we may **gain** a heart of wisdom."

Day 85

God knows where you **hurt.**
God knows where you need to **heal.**
God is a God that **WILL** make you feel
brand new like the first day He knew you.

2 Corinthians 5:17
"Therefore, if anyone is in Christ, the **new** creation has come:
The old has gone, **the new is here**!"

Day 86

Patience will reveal all things.
In time, we will see that what we **wanted**
wasn't what we **needed,** and everything happened the way
it did for a reason.
God has to **make room** for the blessing
He has for you in the next **season.**

Hebrews 10:36
"You need to **persevere** so that when you have done the will of God,
you will receive what He has promised."

Day 87

The **same** way the **enemy** sends people
to **block** your blessings
is the **same** way God sends
people into your **life** from heaven.

Hebrews 6:10
"God is not **unjust**; He will not forget your work
and the love you have shown Him as you have helped His people
and **continue** to help them."

Day 88

When I truly **understood** how God is the **master** of time.
I felt secured in cutting off the wrong men instead of
being **scared** of being lonely.
The one that God has for me **will** meet me,
not too late, nor too early.

Proverbs 16:9
"In their hearts humans **plan** their course,
but the **Lord establishes their step**s."

Day 89

It's so easy to **overlook**
how God is **working** in our lives.
We tend to **forget** that God is **with** us even in the **rain.**
We could have been **burning** in the fire,
but instead we're **alive** to see another day.

2 Thessalonians 1:7
"...and give **relief** to you who are troubled, and to us as well.
This will happen when the Lord Jesus is **revealed from heaven in
blazing fire** with His powerful angels."

Day 90

My breakups **taught** me that **rejection**
is **God's protection.**
Don't place a **comma** where God places a **period.**
He is the **master** of perfection,
His work needs **NO** correction.

1 Peter 2:4
"As you come to Him, the **living Stone** rejected by humans
but chosen by God and precious to Him."

Day 91

You were **born** to be a **warrior,**
not a **worrier.**
For God gave us a spirit not of fear,
but of **power** and **love** and **self-control.**
Therefore, **find** it in your soul
to let anxiety **go.**

1 John 5:4
"For everyone born of God **overcomes** the world.
This is the victory that has overcome the world, even our **faith.**"

Day 92

The reason why **I struggled** for so long
to become **whole and healed**
was because I kept **running** away
from the **season** of **being a caterpillar.**
I was **rushing** to be a butterfly
but **everything** in life goes through cycles
in order to be **transformed.**

2 Corinthians 3:18
"And we all, who with **unveiled faces** contemplate the Lord's glory,
are being **transformed into His image** with ever-increasing glory,
which comes from the Lord, who is the Spirit."

Day 93

As I began to heal and put God in the **center** of my life,
I had to **constantly rewire my mind** to remember
God's words and His promises.
For **so long** I had the enemy in my ear,
who compared to God, is **incompetent.**

1 Peter 1:25
"…but the word of the Lord **endures forever.**"

Day 94

God **never** said the **weapon** wasn't
going to **form**, He said the weapon
wasn't going to **prosper;**
therefore, during the toughest times in your life,
remember that God still is the **comforter
and the doctor.**

Isaiah 54:17
"**No weapon** forged against you will **prevail.**"

Day 95

There are **days** when you may **overthink**
about the future and
what your **life** could turn out to be, but
instead stay **present** and **trust** God's timing.

Isaiah 43:19
"See, I am doing a **new** thing."

Day 96

It's **extremely** important to **heal** before you jump back
into something **new,**
because whether you **realize** it or not,
your heart is vulnerable.
Don't get **caught** up being with the
wrong person because it's **comfortable.**

Jeremiah 33:6
"'Nevertheless, I will **bring health and healing to it; I will heal** my
people and will let them enjoy abundant **peace and security.'"**

Day 97

Tonight, when **I pray**
I will ask God to **provide** me the **strength** to trust Him.
To allow me to not be **fixated** on wanting love,
but to **acknowledge** that His love will **satisfy** all my needs
and that I not a **woman in waiting,**
but a woman with **vision beyond dreams.**

Psalm 27:14
"Wait for the Lord; be **strong** and take **heart**
and **wait for the Lord**."

Day 98

The more I understand my **worth and the vision** that
God has on my life,
the **easier** it is for me to **step** away from
the idea of just wanting to be a wife.

Habakkuk 2:3
"Though it linger, **wait for it;** it will **certainly**
come and **will** not delay."

Day 99

Today I **felt** God's presence in my **heart,**
a feeling I **never** felt before.
It feels like **warm** genuine hugs and **gentle** words of grace.
Your love leaves a taste of **wholeness** with a scent of safety.
God in your presence is where I **want** to be;
a place **forever healed** in your glory.

2 Corinthians 3:17
"Now the **Lord is the Spirit,** and where the Spirit of the Lord is,
there is freedom."

Day 100

Every time I **think** about God's **grace and mercy,**
I become **emotional**
because no matter **how** many times I **disobeyed** God,
He always made sure He was **available**
to come **save me** when I needed **saving.**

Psalm 62:1
"**Truly** my **soul rests** in God; my **salvation** comes from Him."

Day 101

Acknowledge your hurt, your pain, your sorrow,
and **allow** God to help those areas
with His **strength** and love.
For we must **sacrifice** feeling uncomfortable
while God helps us **evolve** into the person
He needs us to **become.**

Psalm 46:1
"God is our **refuge and strength**, an ever-present help in trouble."

Day 102

Repeat these words out loud:
this too shall pass, for **I AM**
Greater than any of my struggles;
Stronger than any of my worries;
Wiser than any of my mistakes;
Smarter than any of my doubts;
I AM a child of the King;
therefore, **I CAN** do anything
through Christ who strengthens me.

Nehemiah 8:10
"Do not grieve, for the **joy** of the Lord is your **strength.**"

Day 103

As the **days** pass,
you'll find your **heart** repairing from the hurt by
becoming **stronger** with each prayer you pray
and with God as your **support.**

Isaiah 46:4
"I will **sustain** you and I will **rescue** you."

Day 104

Just keep in **mind** that the sun doesn't always shine
and just because we don't always **see** it **shining**
doesn't mean it isn't out.
The same way that we may **think** God
isn't **answering** our prayers,
trust me,
He is working it out, **without a doubt.**

2 Samuel 23:4
"He is like the **light of morning** at **sunrise** on a **cloudless morning,**
like the **brightness** after **rain** that brings grass from the earth."

Day 105

It's **not** so much of the relationship
being over that **hurts** the most.
It's the **time**, the **vulnerability**,
the **honesty**, and the **trust** I gave to a person,
to only have been taken **advantage** of in return.
It's the fact that I can **vividly** remember moments when I
sacrificed spending **time** with God,
just to **spend time** with a soul that is nowhere near **capable** of
giving me the **love** that **only** God can supply.
See that's the part that made me cry.

1 John 4:16
"And so, we know and **rely on the love God has for us.**
God is love. Whoever **lives in love lives in God**, and God in them."

Day 106

I always find it **interesting** when people from my **past**
begin to appear in my **present**
because it always makes me **question,**
"Are they **sent** from the enemy or heaven?"

Psalm 119:66
"**Teach me** knowledge and **good judgment**,
for I **trust** Your commands"

Day 107

Time will reveal all things.
No need to **rush** into anything
because the more **patient** you are, the **faster** you'll **see** if
this is a waste of time
or is this a **blessing.**

Luke 8:17
"For there is **nothing hidden** that will not be disclosed,
and nothing concealed that **will not be**
known or brought out into the open."

Day 108

I waited for **four months** to feel how I feel now.
I knew that **within time** my **past** situation wasn't going to
be my **current** situation.
It took me **doing work** to reach this type of **peace** at my
destination.

Proverbs 16:9
"In their **hearts** humans **plan** their course,
but the Lord **establishes** their steps."

Day 109

On your **journey** to healing
you **will** have **moments and days**
when the **enemy** will **test** your disciplinary skills,
because just like God **recognizes** your progress,
the devil does as well.
Except God **guides you** to the gates of heaven
whereas the enemy wants you in **hell.**

Isaiah 58:11
"The LORD will **guide you always;** He will **satisfy your needs in a
sun-scorched land** and will **strengthen** your frame. You will be like a
well-watered garden, like a spring whose waters never fail."

Day 110

We live in a **world** where we are in **constant**
spiritual warfare,
which is why we should **never** underestimate
a **relationship** with God and **faithfulness** to prayer.

2 Thessalonians 3:3
"But the **Lord is faithful,** and He will **strengthen you**
and protect you from the evil one."

Day 111

When I began to **study** Jesus,
I began to have a **better understanding** on what **true
love** entails.
All this time I was sold on the **idea** that love is a **fairytale,**
when in **reality**
love is what Jesus did to save all of humanity.

1 John 4:19
"We **love** because He first **loved** us."

Day 112

When you become more **obedient** to God, you will begin to see how your **wounds** will begin to **heal** at a faster rate. **You do not need** to rely on other **people** to help you escape the hurt and the pain that creeped in that day.

Deuteronomy 5:33
"Walk in **obedience to all that the Lord your God has commanded you**, so that you may **live** and **prosper** and prolong your days in the land that you will possess."

Day 113

With **each day** that passes by,
I **challenge** you to acknowledge God.
Find pockets of **time** to devote to our Heavenly Father,
for He **loves us** so much He gave us
His **one and only** son and left **66 books** behind.
The **least** you can do is give Him your time.

Psalm 90:4
"A **thousand years** in Your sight are like **a day** that has just gone by,
or like a watch in the night."

Day 114

Do not ever **feel** like you're healing **alone**
for God is **always** by your side;
ready to extend His **strength,** pour His **love,** and wrap
His **hands** on your open wounds.
Trust in that through God you will be made brand new.

2 Corinthians 5:17
"Therefore, if anyone is in Christ, **the new creation has come:**
The **old has gone**, the new is here!"

Day 115

God sees it **ALL.**
He sees how **wrong** people did you
and how **much** it hurts;
and because of that we may want **revenge,**
but God wants **transformation;**
not only for your **heart**, but also for them.

Ezekiel 36:26
"I will **give you a new heart** and put a **new spirit** in you;
I will remove **from you your heart of
stone** and give you a heart of flesh."

Day 116

So much **power** comes with being **healed and whole;**
which is why the **enemy** wants you to
continue to be **broken.**
The enemy knows that a **healed person** can only be
healed through **Christ** and God's **wisdom.**
This is why the enemy **never** wants you to heal,
because then you'll become a **threat** to the **Devil's kingdom.**

Ephesians 6:11
"Put on the **full armor of God,** so that you can take your stand
against the devil's schemes."

Day 117

Many of us have experienced **pain and hurt;**
but it doesn't have to **end** there.
There is **joy, peace, and love** in Christ.

Psalm 16:11
"You make known to me the path of life; **You will fill me with joy in
Your presence**, with eternal pleasures at Your right hand."

Day 118

As I continue my **walk** with God,
my desires to lead the path begins to **diminish.**
Each **step** that we take together brings me **closer** to
trusting Him on this journey,
which is why there's no need to **fear or worry.**
When God **orchestrates** your steps
there's no need to rush or hurry
because He knows how to **perfectly** bless your life and
at the same time **receive Glory.**

Ephesians 2:10
"For we are **God's handiwork**, created in Christ Jesus **to do good works**, which God prepared in advance for us to do."

Day 119

My walk with God has **taught** me to not be stingy with
all that I am **learning** about the
Christian faith,
but that I am **obligated** to **share the knowledge** to both
believers and nonbelievers.

2 Corinthians 5:20
"We are therefore Christ's **ambassadors**,
as though God were making His appeal through us.
We implore you on Christ's behalf: Be reconciled to God."

Day 120

I am **training** my mind to remain on **everything**
Kingdom and not of the world.
You see society tries to strip us from the **teachings** of God
since we were **young** boys and girls,
but as I **mature and grow** spiritually in my faith,
I am able to recognize
what's Kingdom and what's of the enemy's place.

Colossians 3:2
"Set your minds on things **above**, NOT on **earthly** things."

Day 121

What happened on the third day?
Jesus **rose**.
God knows that **NO matter** what darkness the enemy
tries to throw your way,
You will **RISE** like the "son".
You may feel **broken**, but my love,
you have **resurrection power**,
a type of **spiritual strength** that no devil can devour.

Philippians 3:9
"and be **found** in Him, not having a righteousness of my own that
comes from the law, but that which
is through faith in Christ—the righteousness that **comes from God**
on the basis of **faith**."

Day 122

The **beautiful** part about life is that **YOU** decide when
your **new** beginning begins.
Every **minute** changes;
Every **hour** is new;
Every **day** is different;
Every **month** resumes.
You decide if you want to **change** or if you want to
remain the same.

Isaiah 60:1
"Arise, shine, **for your light has come**, and the glory of the Lord **rises**
upon you"

Day 123

Our **desires** reside in our heart, which is why our **hearts** can be **deceitful;** because it **allows** our ears to hear what they **want** to hear and our eyes see what they **want** to see. This is why the **Holy Spirit** is an **essential** component to the trinity because the **Spirit of God** guides you, whereas your heart **doesn't always** guide you correctly.

Matthew 6:21
"For where your **treasure** is, there your heart will be also."

Day 124

Many of us are **frustrated** because the **situation** that we are in doesn't look like the **image** we imagined. We allow our **fabricated** expectations to **consume** our imagination verses letting God lead us to our **destination.**

Isaiah 30:21
"Whether you turn to the right or to the left, your **ears** will **hear** a voice behind you, saying, "This is the **way**; walk in it."

Day 125

Today is one of those days, where my cup feels **empty.**
I **spent** a lot of **time** trying to understand
what I don't quite understand.
It's one of those **moments**
when I have to **remind** myself
that God has the whole world in His **hands.**

Proverbs 19:21
"Many are the **plans** in a person's heart,
but it is the Lord's **purpose** that prevails."

Day 126

Before my **walk** with God, I was very **impulsive.** If I
wanted to do something at that **moment**, I did, but now,
that I'm on this **journey** with Christ, **before** I make a
move I think twice.
I ask God to provide me with **confirmation,**
and **show me** if this move is a part of my **destination**.

Proverbs 3:6
"In all your ways **submit to Him**,
and He will make your **paths straight**."

Day 127

One thing that **always** seems to amaze me
is how God always **exceed our expectations.**
See you have a **vision** for yourself,
but God has **visions** for you.
You want that **job,**
but God has a **career.**
You want a **boyfriend/girlfriend,**
but God has a **husband/wife.**
You want **money,**
but God has generational **wealth** attached to your name.
God tells us to **delight ourselves** in Him
and He will **give us** the **desires** of our heart.
Stop trying to do life without God
for when He **created us,** it was to be in **partnership** with
Him, not in separation;
therefore, many of us **ruin** the plan God has for us out of
desperation.

Ephesians 3:20
"Now to Him who is able to do **immeasurably more** than all we ask
or imagine, **according** to His **power** that is at work within us"

Day 128

Many of us are in **spiritual warfare.**
We may think we are **addressing** our issues, but all we are
doing is just **picking** at the fruit
and not at the **root.**
We can **talk** about our **trauma**
and even **address** our **pain,**
but that's just **fruit-based solutions**
that causes the issue to remain.
See when you **align yourself** in Christ, situations that
once pulled you down **begin** to **change**
because the power of God that rebukes the devil,
is in Jesus' name.

Philippians 2:9
"Therefore, God has highly exalted Him and bestowed on Him **the
name that is above every name.**"

Day 129

You **will** come across people who aren't going to **know** your **worth.**
Do not let **you** be one of those people.
Do not **forget** that God knew you **before** you were in your mother's womb.
God made you **fearfully and wonderfully** made.
Those who know that **you are a child** of Christ
will **fear** losing you because of **who you are** and **who you are called to be**.
You were **made** with **purpose**
and **anyone** that tries to belittle you and tell you otherwise
must know the **devil is a liar** and that he can keep his lies.

Jeremiah 1:5
"Before I **formed you in the womb, I knew you**, and before you were born I consecrated you; I appointed you a prophet to the nations."

Day 130

God is **constantly** speaking.
Perhaps you do not **hear** Him because your **flesh** is too
loud, or maybe you
do not spend **enough** alone time with Him to even
recognize how He **communicates** with you.
I know for me, before building my relationship with God,
I remember **overlooking** the signs God would **send** me,
but now I **eagerly** seek God's voice and
recognize when He is calling me to **listen** in closely.

John 10:27
"My sheep **listen to My voice;** I know them, and they **follow** Me."

Day 131

I **never** want to **experience** another broken heart.
The **pain** and **hurt** that came from desiring **a person**
more than I desired **God**
is a **situation** I want to **avoid** at all cost.
I recognize that **NO one** outside of God
can **supply** His type of **love.**
It may **feel** like you're **winning** with **temporary** pleasures,
but when it's not God **ordained**, then it's a loss.

Psalm 136:26
"Give **thanks** to the God of heaven. His love **endures** forever."

Day 132

Taking a leap in **faith** means **walking** in faith
and not by sight.
God will tell you to **step** into something
that does not **always**
look nor **sound right,**
but are you going to **miss** His blessing because
you are afraid to **trust** His word?
Or are you going to
take that **leap in faith**
because of the **word** you heard from God?

Romans 10:17
"Consequently, **faith** comes from **hearing** the message, and the
message is heard through the word about Christ."

Day 133

One of the **many** things I've learned on this **journey**
to **becoming** whole through Christ is
recognizing the season.
Mislabeling your season will have you entertaining
the wrong people for no reason.
See, I had to **recognize** that right now
I'm **under construction** and right now
God **needs** all my energy.
Entertaining what God did not send
will be an **interruption**
to what God wants to **produce in me**.

Proverbs 16:3
"**Commit** to the Lord whatever you do, and He will **establish** your
plans."

Day 134

Those **small** red flags that you recognize in the beginning
but **ignore** will **never** turn green.
These flags are a lot more **dangerous**
than what they appear to be.
In **time** those red flags get **larger** in size.
Honey, don't wait to **realize** when
God is **sending** you a sign.
Address God in prayer and He'll help **open** your eyes.

Psalm 146:8
"The Lord gives **sight** to the **blind**, the Lord **lifts up** those who are
bowed down, the Lord loves the righteous."

Day 135

When you **understand** the **value** God has given you,
there is **no** way that you can begin to
value yourself as anything **less.**
When you **understand** the purpose
that God has **assigned** to your name,
then you will begin to **walk**
with a certain type of **confidence** on your chest.
You **recognize** who makes the shots and calls so nobody,
not man, not woman can make you **stumble or fall.**

Romans 8:31
"What, then, shall we say in response to these things?
If God **is for us,** who can be **against us**?"

Day 136

As you heal, don't forget to **forgive yourself**
for your **past** behaviors.
Today I had to recognize that I was still **holding** on to
hurt from my past **failures.**
Failure of recognizing my **value** and my **worth**,
because I **idolize** being in a relationship with a man
instead of seeking a relationship God **formed**
with me **since** birth.

Psalm 46:5
"God is **within her**; she will not fall;
God will **help her at break of day.**"

Day 137

Before knowing my purpose,
I realize that I didn't **value** my time.
I used to **pour** too much of myself into **empty** cups.
But now, I've **learned** where to draw the line.

Galatians 6:5
"For **each one** should carry their **own** load."

Day 138

God works in **mysterious** ways.
He is always **listening and working**
even on the **hardest** days.
Cast your **fears** at His **feet** and **continue**
to give Him **praise**
because He is a God that **never fails,**
but **continues** to amaze.

Psalm 55:22
"**Cast your cares on the Lord,** and He will **sustain you;**
He will **never** let the righteous be shaken."

Day 139

Not only is God a God that **heals,**
He is also a God that **feels.**
He knows what **hurts** you.
He knows what makes you **cry.**
He knows what makes you **smile** and how you **feel** inside.
However, He still **wants** you to tell Him how you feel in
prayer because He is the **ultimate healer and repairer.**

Jeremiah 17:14
"**Heal me, Lord,** and **I will be healed**; save me and I will be saved,
for You are the one I praise."

Day 140

I **find** that even when I **delight myself** in the Lord,
it's still a challenge trying to **balance** the **spiritual** with
the **physical** world.
So, when I feel like I'm **losing grip** on God,
I **turn** and **open** the manual because **reading** God's words
brings me back to **center** place
where God and I
can be **back** on the **same** pace.

Isaiah 2:5
"Let us **walk** in the **light** of the Lord."

Day 141

I can't lie, these **past** couple of **days**
I feel like I have been **battling**
with the **old** me,
the me that would get **caught up** on what **could** be.
I **don't** want to take **life** into my own
hands, because of **anxiety**
So, I just **continue** to **pray** to
God for **clarity.**

Psalm 119:130
"The unfolding of Your words gives **light**;
it gives **understanding** to the simple."

Day 142

Today was **tough**.
Today reminded me that I **still** have that part of me
that gets too **caught** up
on **fantasy** instead of **reality**.
I'm currently **struggling** with **following** God's strategy.
Just **wish** He can **audibly** tell me whether or not
the men that pursue me are the men
that's truly **meant** for me,
or are they just trying to **distract** me.

1 Corinthians 7:35
"I am saying this for your own **good,** not to **restrict** you, but that you
may **live** in a right way in **undivided** devotion to the Lord."

Day 143

Anytime you're **desperate** you'll always **confuse** God's
red flags as a **green light.**
This is why **healing** and **understanding**
that God is the **source** to
solving **all** your **problems** is **important**
because it **saves** you from seeking
comfort from the serpent.

Psalm 62:1
"Truly my **soul** finds rest in God; my **salvation** comes from Him."

Day 144

This journey has **taught** me that **love** will find you.
There is **no** need to go **chasing** after **Love**.
Before I had a "F.O.M.O" (fear of missing out) complex,
but now I **recognize** that **fear** and **faith** can't **coexist.** So,
the challenge is **trusting** the process
even when the man of my **dreams** seems not to exist.

Jeremiah 17:7
"But **blessed** is the one who **trusts** in the Lord,
whose **confidence** is in Him."

Day 145

Today I **reflected** on the past
and **realized** that there's still a lot
of work in me that **needs** to be done.
God, I ask that you **make** me **whole** again.
Pick up my **broken pieces** and allow me to be one.
I no **longer** want tiny **scattered** pieces
spread out on **wooden** floors.
God, I ask that you **heal** me
because I'm **completely** all yours.

Hebrews 13:5
"Never will I **leave** you; never will I **forsake** you."

Day 146

Depression is **real** and so is **God**.
Prayer is our weapon
and **counseling** is a method to **climbing** out
of the **dark** place
you have been trying to **find** light.
God **speaks** to us **through** others.
Seeking **therapy** may be **exactly** what you need.
Never **underestimate** the **power** of Jesus and therapy.

Proverbs 11:14
"For lack of **guidance** a nation falls, but **victory**
is won through many advisers."

Day 147

Transitioning is hard.
It **knocks** you out of rhythm,
disrupts your **momentum,** and **interrupts** your flow, but
I believe God allows us to **experience** transitions,
so we don't get **comfortable** with where we are and
where God wants us to go.
So, no matter how hard **transitioning** feels,
remember that God is by your side, so just **go** with His flow.

Psalm 37:23
"The Lord makes **good** the steps of the one who delights in Him."

Day 148

There are **times** when I just **pause** and
thank God for His
Grace;
Mercy;
Love;
Patience;
and, most **importantly His healing powers.**
He makes me **feel whole** again.
God, You're the one relationship
I don't **ever** want to end.

Psalm 86:15
"But You, Lord, are a **compassionate** and **gracious** God,
slow to anger, **abounding** in love and **faithfulness.**"

Day 149

God, I **need** You, my **heart** is **still hurting.**
I still feel **broken**, my father has caused me
so much **pain**. I ask that You come **take it away.**
Remove every **hurtful** word he told me.
I **thought** I was doing the **right** thing
by reaching out to him and **trying** to make
things work, but my dad **always** makes me feel worse.
For the person who is reading this, just know
that healing is not a **destination,** it's a **journey.**
So, when you **experience** moments of depression,
acknowledge your hurt and give yourself **mercy.**
Remember how worthy this walk with God is for
it is the **building** blocks to your recovery.

Joshua 1:9
"Have I not commanded you? Be **strong** and **courageous.**
Do not be afraid; do not be discouraged,
for the Lord your God **will** be with you **wherever** you go."

Day 150

God, at times it feels like **maybe** You are too busy
to **make** a way when it feels like there is **no** way;
but then I **remember** that You are God.
A God that is **faithful, trustworthy, and omniscient.**
Even when its feels like you're absent, just **closing** my eyes
and **inviting** You into my space is **sufficient** enough to
know You're **present.**

Exodus 34:6
"And he passed in front of Moses, proclaiming,
"The Lord, the Lord, the **compassionate** and **gracious** God,
slow to anger, abounding in love and faithfulness"

Day 151

I **realized** that in order to **fully** heal,
I have to **cut off** the **wires** that gave
power to my pain.
At the **same** time being okay
with knowing that **nothing** will ever
remain the same.

Hebrews 6:19
"We have this **hope** as an **anchor** for the soul, firm and secure.
It enters the **inner** sanctuary behind the curtain"

Day 152

Never **confuse adjusting** to **healing**
because it **leads** to spilling
your pain on others.
Instead, **comfort** what you try to **cover**
and let God **help** you **discover**
what you **need** to be whole again.

Jeremiah 30:17
"But I will **restore** you to **health** and **heal** your wounds,'
declares the Lord"

Day 153

The **weight** from the world is **heavy.**
No one expected what we **experienced** in 2020.
There is a war outside **larger** than what the eyes can see.
It goes beyond a **pandemic** and police **brutality.**
This is **spiritual warfare** and
many people are **awakening.**
God, I just **pray** that you bring **healing**
to everything that is happening.

1 John 4:4
"You, dear children, are from God and have **overcome them**, because
the one who is **in you** is **greater** than the **one** who **is in the world.**"

Day 154

Set your **mind** on **all** things **above**
and **not** on **earthly** things.
When I **find** myself feeling **anxious,**
it is due to my mind **focusing**
on the **world** instead of on God.
When I **switch** my focus and get in God's **presence,**
my **present** state becomes a place of peace.

1 Corinthians 6:14
"By His power God **raised** the Lord from the **dead**,
and He will **raise** us also."

Day 155

As of **lately** I feel as though God and I
are **not** on the **same** pace.
I've been too **busy** trying to **keep up** with the world that
I have **lost** my **place** walking **beside** God.
Tomorrow is another day to **remind** myself to **slow down**
because not being in the presence of God makes me feel
like God is **nowhere** to be found.

Colossians 2:6
"So then, just as you **received** Christ Jesus as Lord,
continue to live your lives in Him"

Day 156

God, I pray for **clarity** and **wisdom;**
I pray for **freedom.**
Freedom **for all** and **all;**
freedom from **injustice** to **sin.**
I know I have to **trust** Your timing,
because Your **timing** is perfect.
You always know when to **chime** in,
even in **moments** when my **patience** is running thin.

Psalm 130:5
"I **wait** for the Lord, my whole being waits,
and in His **word** I put my hope."

Day 157

It's **hard** being in this world and **not** of this world.
The **same** way it's hard to **set** the **mind** on things **above**
instead of things on **earth**
because so much of our **identity** has
been **socially constructed.**
But what I am **realizing** is that
when I do bring the parts of myself
created from God to the **forefront** of my mind, I can
decline feelings of inadequacy.
For I am reminded that I am **created**
in the **image** of God.

John 17:16
"**They** are not of the world, even as **I am not of it.**"

Day 158

There are days I am **reminded**
of **hope** and **restoration**
knowing that **healing** takes **patience**
and with patience comes the **fruition** of our **affirmations.**

Psalm 16:9
"Therefore, my **heart** is glad and my **tongue** rejoices;
my **body** also will rest secure."

Day 159

Each day is a **gift,**
an **unwrapped** present we sometimes take for **granted.**
I ask that God **continues** to keep me planted,
watered with the Holy Spirit,
and nourished with the "Son".
I give **thanks** for each day that has begun.

Psalm 118:24
"The Lord has done it this very day; let us **rejoice** today and **be glad**"

Day 160

God, could it be that you're **speaking,**
but because You're not speaking what we **prefer,**
we **believe** that you are not speaking at all.
God, I ask that You provide me the **strength**
to stay **strong** and not fall
as I **wait** for your confirmation
on the word you want **delivered** to me.
I know that I am on this walk.
I **vowed** to practice waiting patiently.

James 5:8
"You too, **be patient** and **stand firm,**
because the Lord's **coming** is near."

Day 161

It's funny because you **never** know
God's plan
until you're **living** it out;
which, is why we should **walk** by faith
and not with **doubt.**

Hebrews 11:6
"And **without** faith it is **impossible** to please God,
because anyone who comes to Him must
believe that He **exists** and that He **rewards**
those who **earnestly** seek Him."

Day 162

Sometimes I have to **ask** myself,
"God is this You or is this a **distraction?**"
See it's so hard to **distinguish** the two
when there's an **attraction.**
I keep asking God to **guide** my steps
and **help me** stay **focused** on Him
because ultimately taking my eyes **off** God
is the quickest way to fall into temptation or sin.

Psalm 1:2
"But whose **delight** is in the law of the Lord, and who **meditates** on
His law day and night."

Day 163

A **faithful** God.
A God that is in **control** even when **everything** around
me feels chaotic.
Thank you, God.
For **always** being by my side even **during** times when I
feel like I want **to hide** and **cry.**
You **continue** to show me
that when I **include** you in the **picture**
the outcome is always 3 times **better** and **sweeter.**

Colossians 3:17
"And whatever you do, whether in **word** or **deed,**
do it all in the **name of the Lord Jesus**, giving
thanks to God the Father through Him."

Day 164

God, I **call** on You because
I know that I **need** Your **strength** to rub on me.
It's **hard** being in the flesh.
I need You to **guide** me **daily**.
Please Lord, provide me with **discernment** and **clarity**.

Exodus 15:2
"The Lord is my **strength** and my **defense**,
He has become my **salvation**."

Day 165

Our **father** who **art** in heaven **please** come down to **earth**
and give me my **daily** bread;
because as of lately, **parts** of me are
beginning to feel **dead.**
God, why do they keep **killing** people that **look** like me?
God, I ask that you help **heal ALL** of humanity.

Matthew 6:10
"Your kingdom come, Your will be **done,** on **earth** as it is in **heaven.**"

Day 166

The **air** feels **thick**
like **pages stacked** in the **bible.**
These past few **months** feel like we are on trial.
God, what is it that **You** want **us** to do,
because I would do **anything** for you.

Psalm 50:15
"and **call on Me** in the day of trouble; I will **deliver** you,
and you will **honor** Me."

Day 167

Today is my **dad's** birthday;
however, we **do not** speak, but I **still** pray that God
touches his heart
and makes it **softer** than bed sheets.
The **hurt** he caused runs **deep,**
but God only you know exactly what **he and I need.**

Philippians 4:19
"And my God will **meet all your needs** according to the
riches of his **glory** in Christ Jesus."

Day 168

God, Your **love** is like no other
and there is **no other love** I rather **receive.**
You **help guide,** balance, and **strengthen** me
which is why I will **forever** serve You,
now and **eternally.**

Exodus 15:2
"The Lord is my **strength** and my **defense**;
He has become my salvation."

Day 169

God, although You tell us to **cast** our **fears** at Your feet,
I still find it hard for my **heart** and **mind** to meet.
My **heart** contains Your **words,**
but my **mind** knows what it **sees**
and a lot of **times** the **fear** of what I see
makes it hard to **believe;**
so, when I have **moments** like these
I **ask,** "Lord please
strengthen me with Your **spirit**
so that my **mind** can be **free.**

Galatians 5:1
"It is for **freedom** that Christ has set us **free. Stand firm**, then, and
do not **let yourselves be burdened** again by a **yoke** of slavery."

Day 170

And after it **rains,** You bring out the **sun;**
and after the **storm,** You bring out the **light;**
and after the **fire,** You bring out the **water;**
and after the **pain,** You bring **sight;**
and after **conviction,** You bring the **altar;**
and after all, You still **restore;**
because, You are a God that's **bigger** and **more**
than **anything** we can endure.

Job 26:14
"And these are but the outer fringe of His works; how **faint** the
whisper we hear of Him! Who then can understand
the **thunder** of His **power?"**

Day 171

If there is **anything** you **pray** for tonight,
let it be **wisdom.**
The more I became an **open** book for God,
the more the **word** of God **became** more than a **book**
protecting me from getting **caught up**
in the enemy's hook.

Ephesians 5:15-16
"Be very careful, then, how you live—not as **unwise** but as **wise,**
making the most of every **opportunity,** because the days are evil."

Day 172

God, only You **know** my future,
only You **direct** my path,
only You **know** my desires,
and things I must **let go** and the things I can **have.**
I just ask that You **guide** me and that I am **always**
walking in Your **will** even if that means
I **need** to **sit back** and **remain still.**

Isaiah 30:21
"Whether you turn to the **right** or to the **left,** your ears will **hear** a
voice behind you, saying, "**This is the way; walk in it.**""

Day 173

Help me **guard** my heart
because I fall in **love** so easily.
Fall for the **thought** of everything we can **possibly** be, but
putting God first **helps** with **removing** my heart from my
sleeve, because God **provides** me
with **discernment** and **clarity.**

Galatians 5:16
"So, I say, walk by the **Spirit,** and You will not **gratify**
the desires of the **flesh**."

Day 174

When you **transition** into the kingdom
you may begin to **struggle** with what you **used** to do
from what you **need** to do.
When you're in God's **presence,**
surround yourself with **people** on the same **journey**
because being **surrounded** by non kingdom citizens can
shift the **trajectory** of your story.

Proverbs 12:26
"The **righteous** choose their friends carefully,
but the way of the **wicked** leads them astray."

Day 175

Thank You, Lord, for **helping** me **heal** my heart.
Thank You for not **allowing** us to do life **alone.**
Thank You for Your **grace** and Your **mercy.**
You **deserve** all of the praise and glory.

Psalm 7:17
"I will give **thanks** to the Lord because of His **righteousness**;
I will sing the **praises** of the name of the
Lord Most High."

Day 176

I don't want to **fall** into being a **victim** for doing so much
for Jesus,
yet spend **no time** with Jesus.
God, I want to **be** at Your **feet** daily
and daily I **will** be at Your feet.

Matthew 15:30
"Great crowds came to Him, bringing the **lame**, the **blind,**
the **crippled**, the **mute** and many others,
and **laid** them at His **feet**; and **He healed them.**"

Day 177

God already **confirmed** your life
the **minute** you were born.
Already gave you **dominion** to **shine** your **light** in rooms
that you **never** thought you'll be in.
Walk through doors with your head **high**
and your **faith** even **higher,**
because God is the **ultimate** qualifier
and baby you're **qualified.**

2 Corinthians 3:5
"Not that we are **competent** in **ourselves**
to claim **anything** for ourselves,
but our **competence** comes from God."

Day 178

The enemy loves to **present** itself
in **pleasurable** things
because it **knows** the **desires** of your heart;
but **prayer** and time will **reveal** all that you **need** to know.
Don't **rush**, take things **slow**.
Use **wisdom** to help **discern**
what **stays** and what you **need** to let **go.**

James 1:5
"If any of you **lacks** wisdom, you should ask God, who **gives**
generously to all **without** finding fault,
and it will be **given** to you."

Day 179

It's **important** to know what **season**
God has placed you in,
so that you know how to best **serve** in that season.
If God **wants** you to be single and focused on Him
then **be** single and focus on God.
Not **serving** your **season** properly
will only **prolong** the season you do not
necessarily want to be in.
Hang in there and **trust** God's timing.

Lamentations 3:25
"The Lord is **good** to those whose **hope** is in Him,
to the **one** who seeks Him."

Day 180

There are some **lessons** that God
wants to **teach** you that can only
be **taught** in your **single** season.
So if you are single I **challenge** you to **accomplish**
all that God has **called** you to and really dive into
learning more about who you are
while you **wait** and **enjoy** the waiting room of your **blessing.**"

Colossians 1:10
"…so that you may live a **life worthy** of the Lord and **please Him** in
every way: **bearing** fruit in every
good work, **growing** in the knowledge of God."

Day 181

God will send people to help you; the **enemy** will send people to help you.
And the **Holy Spirit** of God will be there to help you; help you **discern** God from the enemy which is why we must **pray** and **ask** God for **clarity.**

Psalm 119:130
"The unfolding of Your words **gives light**;
it gives understanding to the **simple**."

Day 182

Only God **knows** what you been **through**
and He is an **expert** in **repairing** hearts.
Whatever open **wound** you have that still **stings**, let God
be the **one** to tell you it will be okay,
and within **time**, you will begin to **realize** that
you walked into healing as the **night** became **night**
and the **day** became **day.**

Psalm 34:18
"The Lord is close to the **brokenhearted** and **saves** those who are
crushed in spirit."

Day 183

Don't **give up** on your walk.
Look how **far** you have **made** it.
With **each** step you take with Jesus is a step **closer**
to your breakthrough.
You are the one that's going to **break**
the generational **curse.**
You are the one that's going to **create** generational **wealth.**
Your **breakthrough** is tied to **freeing** your bloodline;
So, **cry** if you have to, but there's **no giving up** this time.

1 Corinthians 16:13
"Be on your **guard**; stand firm in the **faith**;
be **courageous**; be **strong.**"

Day 184

You may **weep** at **night,**
but there will be **joy** in the **morning.**
It may **pour** on your **parade,**
but there will be **sunshine** later in the **day.**
You're **hurting** now,
but you'll be **healed** later.
The type of God I **serve** is so much **greater** than
anything you will experience.

Psalm 147:5
"Great is our **Lord** and **mighty** in power;
His understanding has **no limit**".

Day 185

Don't **listen** to your **heart,**
listen to your **spirit.**
The **heart** is **deceitful** and **heightens** our **own** desires.
Rely on the **Holy Spirit** who's
wisdom never expires.

Galatians 5:25
"Since we **live** by the **Spirit**, let us keep in **step** with the **Spirit.**"

Day 186

You'll **never** truly know the God that is a **waymaker** until you are in the **pit** of a **valley looking** for a way **out** of an **impossible** situation.
Only to find out that God **led** you to that **destination** to experience how **faith** in God
sparks the fire of miracles.

Acts 4:30
"Stretch out Your hand to **heal** and **perform signs** and **wonders** through the name of Your Holy servant Jesus."

Day 187

Walking with God doesn't **exempt** you from
experiencing hardship.
What it does is **provide** peace
that **suppresses** your **understanding.**

Philippians 4:7
"And the **peace** of God, which **transcends** all understanding,
will **guard your hearts** and your **minds** in Christ Jesus."

Day 188

I **challenge** you to **let go** of your **past** sins.
Remind the devil that he will **not** win.
That God **loves** us so much He **wrapped** Himself in **flesh**
and **washed** us clean with the blood of Jesus.
I will not make the **same** mistakes.
Instead I will **learn** and **grow** from every season.

1 Corinthians 15:3
"For what I **received** I **passed** on to you as of first **importance:** that
Christ **died** for our sins according to the scriptures."

Day 189

When **pain** meets you, it for sure **changes** you.
It may **swallow** you up like
life does to **dreams**
or **set** you on **fire**
like **burning** trees;
but as you are going **through**
your **wilderness** season,
continuously seek God and **keep believing.**

John 7:38
"Whoever **believes in Me**, as scripture has said,
rivers of **living water** will **flow** from within them."

Day 190

Celebrate the "No's"
because "No" means that
there is something **bigger** and **better**
that God has in **store** for you.
You may **think** this is what you want **now,** but my love,
God has something **special** and **significant**
waiting at a new door for you.

1 Corinthians 2:9
"What no **eye** has seen, what no **ear** has heard, and what no **human
mind** has conceived, the things God has **prepared**
for those who love Him."

Day 191

It's funny how **one** day you'll wake up
and notice your **spirit** has **returned** back to you.
Not the spirit of **fear, worry, and anxiety,**
but the spirit God has **placed** in you since birth.
The spirit that is **linked** to **breaking**
the generational curse.

Acts 2:4
"**All** of them were **tied** with the Holy Spirit and began
to **speak** in other tongues as the **Spirit** enabled them."

Day 192

God **already** knows the **beginning,** the **middle,**
and the **end** of our story
and because we don't,
we tend to get **anxious** and begin to **worry.**
You're a child of God, **continue** to **read** the **bible** and
seek His presence.
He is going to **lead** you to glory
just **count** your **blessings.**

Psalm 25:4-5
"**Guide** me in Your **truth** and **teach** me, for You are God my **Savior,**
and my **hope** is in You all day long."

Day 193

You are **beautiful** and **full** of life
and as you **live** in this world
you'll **quickly** learn how people will try to **quiet** your
fame and **dim** your **light,**
and **through it all** you are **given** a **choice**
to choose the **voice** you want to believe.
Your **identity** is not wrapped up
in the **broken** package of **society,**
but it is **sampled** and **sealed** by God's hands
and the more your **relationship** grows with God,
the more that is a **concept** you'll **understand.**

Ephesians 1:4
"For He **chose** us in Him **before** the **creation** of the world
to be **holy** and **blameless** in His sight. In love."

Day 194

We all **heard** the **saying** "time heals all wounds,"
but what if I told you that it was **never** the time
that healed you, but it was the **ticking** of God's love that
sealed your open cuts.
And as the **seconds** turned to **minutes,**
and the **minutes** turned to **hours,**
God **poured** into you like
summer **rain** on dried out flowers.

Psalm 147:3
"He **heals** the **brokenhearted** and **binds** up their wounds."

Day 195

God is a God that **keeps** His promises;
However, you'll **never** know the promises
until you get to know **Him.**
You'll **never** get to the **promises** until
you **commit** your **heart** and **soul** to Him
like He did for you.

2 Peter 3:18
"But **grow** in the **grace** and **knowledge** of our Lord and Savior Jesus
Christ. To Him be glory both **now** and **forever!** Amen."

Day 196

It's **liberating** to know that
God **provides**, God **restores**, God **heals**
and does so much more.
Put your **trust** in God and He **will** guide you to
nothing but **open** doors.

Psalm 34:10
"The lions may **grow** weak and hungry, but those who **seek**
the Lord **lack no good** thing."

Day 197

On this **journey** I had to **understand**
to **choose purpose** over **preference.**
Many times, we **allow** the **desires** of our hearts
to **get in the way** of our blessing.

Proverbs 8:10
"Choose my **instruction** instead of silver, **knowledge**
rather than choice gold."

Day 198

God **cannot** bless who you **pretend** to be.
Show Him your **open wounds,** your **unhealed cuts**, and your **brokenness**
so that He can **pour** into those **areas**
and **provide** you the **wisdom** and the **strength** you need
to **become** the person, you are **called** to be.

Psalm 26:4
"I do not sit with the **deceitful**, nor do I **associate** with hypocrites."

Day 199

In this **world,** you will **constantly** have to remind
yourself who you are and who you belong to.
You are a **child** of God;
A blessing; A prayer;
A **creation** created by the utmost **creator.**
Don't let **society** tell you **otherwise**
and don't you **dare** fall for the devil's lies.

Genesis 1:27
"So, God **created** mankind **in His own image**, in the image of God
He **created** them; male and female He created them."

Day 200

There will be **days** when the **gap** between
you and **Jesus** feel as though it has **widened**
due to the **distractions** that **appears**
as you take steps to have Jesus **near.**
The enemy **loves** to **separate** us,
but do not **allow** your **flesh** to be **weak** by
the **distorted** images the enemy wants us to **seek;**
instead steadfast to the Lord and **listen** when He speaks.

Psalm 119:15
"I **meditate** on Your **precepts** and **consider** Your ways."

Day 201

There isn't a day that goes by that I
do not **consciously** kill my flesh.
For so long, I **thought negatively** about death,
but **everything** that lives, dies
and that's not **always** a bad thing.

John 3:30
"He must become **greater**; I must become **less**."

Day 202

God tells us to **delight** ourselves in Him
and He will **give** us the **desires** of our heart.
God is **waiting** for **us** to **commit** to **Him** to bring us to the **promise**
He is **waiting** for us to **receive.**
Many times we get **wrapped** up in our **disbelief,**
wondering how **something** so **good** and so **great** can happen to me.
The God that we **serve** looks **past** your **imperfections**
once we trade in our hearts for His perfections.
There is no **stopping** His plan or changing His mind,
God loves you, just trust His time.

Romans 15:13
"May the God of hope fill you with all **joy** and **peace**
as you **trust** in Him, so that you may **overflow**
with **hope** by the **power** of the Holy Spirit."

Day 203

We act like we are **doing** God a **favor**
when we **live** a **righteous** life;
however, God did us a **favor** when He **wrapped** Himself
in **flesh** and **covered us** with His blood
for our **salvation.**
The least we can do is **commit** to His
ways **without** hesitation.

1 Kings 8:61
"And may your hearts be fully **committed** to the Lord our God, to
live by His **decrees** and obey His **commands**, as at this time."

Day 204

When **walking** with God, **your** desires
and **God's** desires **need** to align,
or else there will be a **constant** battle between
your **heart** and your **mind;**
however, the more **time** you **spend** with God,
the more you will **begin** to want all that He wants for you
even when it's not the **initial** desire you wanted to pursue.

Psalm 40:8
"I **desire** to do Your will, my God, Your law is **within** my heart."

Day 205

One of the **greatest** gifts that God has given
humanity is **identity.**
God **identifies** us as **image bearers** who are **fearfully**
and **wonderfully** made.
However, **society** tries to **define** us **outside** of God's
definition of who we **truly** are.
You my love, are God's **precious** star.
An **impeccable, unblemished, pristine** being
from the **simple** fact that you are **created** in God's image
one of humanity's **greatest** privilege.

2 Corinthians 9:15
"**Thanks** be to God for His **indescribable** gift."

Day 206

During my **process** of **healing**
I've learned that you **grow** through what you **go** through,
which is the **beauty** of all **challenges** faced in life.
Growth at times can be **uncomfortable** like wet socks on
cold evenings, similar to when babies are teething, but
growth is a feeling **worth** feeling
whether you are **still** hurt or in the **process** of healing.

1 Peter 2:3
"Now that you have **tasted** that the Lord is good."

Day 207

God, **today**
I pray for the **lukewarm** Christians.
I pray for the **hurt** Christians and **non**-Christians.
I ask that You **open** their **spiritual** eyes and hearts
to **accepting** You and all of Your parts.

Ephesians 6:18
"And **pray** in the Spirit on all **occasions** with all **kinds** of **prayers**
and **requests**. With this in mind, be **alert**
and **always** keep on **praying** for all the Lord's people."

Day 208

It's easy to **praise** God when our **flowers** are **watered** and
our **cups** overflow,
but are you **able** to **praise** God when **storms** invade your
peace, and the **lights** go **out** during your show?
Are you able to **praise** God when the **blessings** roll in
slower than you **expected** it to go?

Psalm 35:28
"My **tongue** will **proclaim** Your **righteousness**,
Your **praises** all day long."

Day 209

You have to **prepare** for the blessing
before receiving the blessing.
Some of the **blessings** that God wants to **bless** you with
weighs tons of pounds;
However, if you are not **spiritually** fit,
you will have your **blessing** slip
right from your fingertips.

Proverbs 21:31
"The horse is **made** ready for the day of battle,
but **victory rests** with the Lord."

Day 210

So many people want **freedom,**
but yet they are in **bondage** to pornography, lust, drugs,
alcohol, and much more.
The **plan** that God has for you **requires** you to close
the door on the **chapter** with the **character**
of who you **used** to be,
because **walking** with God **requires**
transformative energy.

John 8:36
"So, if the **Son sets you free**, you will be **free indeed.**"

Day 211

Pressure is **precious.**
She is to be **handled** with care.
Ignore her and you may **begin** to feel her **wrath;**
embrace her and you may be **able** to **tackle** the task.
But with it all, ask God to **provide** you with **wisdom**
on how not to **stumble** or **fall**
when **pressure** begins to call.

2 Corinthians 4:8
"We are hard **pressed** on every side, but not **crushed; perplexed,**
but not in **despair.**"

Day 212

Trusting **yourself** can be foolish,
but **wisdom** is wise
the same way
that **trusting** your **heart** is **deceiving**
and it can **feed** your **mind** lies.
God tells us to **not** lean on our own **understanding,**
but to **trust** in Him no matter
what we see with our **eyes.**

2 Corinthians 5:7
"For we **live** by **faith**, not by **sight**."

Day 213

Healing is an **unpredictable** journey
to being **whole** again.
No one tells you how the **process** is unstable.
Some days you'll feel like you **can** move **mountains,** while
other days you'll feel like you're **drowning;**
but, through it all you're **surrounded** by God's **presence,**
He just has to be invited.

Psalm 145:18
"The Lord is **near** to all who **call** on Him,
to all who **call** on Him in **truth.**"

Day 214

Feelings are **excellent** servants and **terrible** masters.
As you **walk** with God, you **must** learn to **quiet** your
thoughts and **focus** on what
feelings are deceiving.
Your **spirit** is worth **believing.**

Romans 8:14
"For those who are **led** by the **Spirit** of God
are the **children** of God."

Day 215

Progression over **perfection.**
Always **strive** for better
and remember to be **patient** with yourself.

Galatians 6:9
"Let us not become **weary** in doing **good,** for at the **proper** time
we will **reap** a harvest if we do not give up."

Day 216

Learn to **quiet** your **insecurities.**
Your **trauma** will try to **drown** out your **healing**
and when you **begin** feeling like your **own voice** is on
mute, pray to God and **let** Him **substitute**
your **emptiness** with His **wholeness.**

Isaiah 65:24
"Before they **call,** I will **answer;** while they are still **speaking,**
I will hear."

Day 217

Be **patient** with **yourself,**
great things **always** take time.
Don't let what you **can't** control **interfere**
with what God has
already **assigned** to your name.

Psalm 126:3
"The Lord has done **great** things for us, and we are filled with joy."

Day 218

We must **learn** to step out of our **picture**
and **view** our situation
with a **fresh** pair of **eyes,**
asking ourselves **questions**
we **answered** with lies.
When we step out of our **picture,** we then can **recognize**
that we have **replaced** God's **image** for a
minimized version of what
God has **envisioned** for our lives.

Psalm 33:11
"But the **plans** of the Lord stand **firm** forever, the **purposes**
of His **heart** through all generations."

Day 219

Appreciate the rain when the **skies** are gray
because in order to **grow,**
raindrops need to flow.

1 Thessalonians 5:18
"Give thanks in **all** circumstances;
for this is God's **will** for you in Christ Jesus."

Day 220

You are greater than your **doubts,**
greater than your **trauma,**
greater than your **pain,**
and **all** of life's drama.
You are greater than your **insecurities,**
greater than your **mistakes.**
You are worthy of God's love and all of His grace.

Philemon 1:25
"The **grace** of the Lord Jesus Christ **be** with your spirit."

Day 221

Each day is a **blessing** and an **opportunity**
to laugh harder,
to be **wiser,**
and make **smarter** choices.
Each day is an **opportunity** to **quiet** the voices
and choose God **throughout** each **moment.**

1 John 4:8
"Whoever does not **love** does not **know** God, because God is love."

Day 222

When you do not **properly** heal, you **allow** your
insecurities to **settle** in the driver's seat
never allowing your **feet** to settle **down** on concrete,
never allowing you to ever
feel **grounded;**
to feel **whole,**
to feel **relieved,**
from past **trauma** that doesn't want to leave;
but God **loves** you very much
and is **able** to fill **every** void.
Set **yourself** in the **presence** of God
and **watch** you meet joy.

Psalm 16:11
"You make **known** to me the **path** of life; You will **fill me** with **joy** in
Your presence, with eternal **pleasures** at Your right hand."

Day 223

The **hardest** part **always** seems to last **forever**
as if someone magically **paused** time
and **froze** the **moments** that made you smile;
but, the Son of God **can** melt **away** your **concerns**
and **turn** your **pain** into **purpose.**
So, keep on **praying** and **never** grow hopeless.

Psalm 31:24
"Be **strong** and take **heart**, all you who **hope** in the Lord."

Day 224

Relationships are **critical** to our development
as they can **gear** us **to** or **away** from God.
The devil is a **deceiver** who **deceives** everyone,
even believers.
It is **important** to use **wisdom, discernment,**
and **prayer** daily
for our **physical** and **spiritual** safety.

Proverbs 13:20
"**Walk** with the wise and **become** wise, for a **companion** of fools
suffers harm."

Day 225

God tells us to love our **neighbors** as we love **ourselves**,
but what **ends** up happening
is that we end up loving ourselves in a **broken way**,
extending that same love to our neighbors.

Matthew 22:39
"And the second is like it: 'Love your neighbor as yourself'"

Day 226

This world has **mastered** how to **alter** your **identity** to
allow you to **portray** a false sense of **who** you truly are.
Honey **never** lose **sight** of who God has **called** you to be.
Remember you are in this world **and** not of it.
So, **don't** look to the crowd, but **above** it.

Ephesians 5:8
"For you were once **darkness**, but now you are **light** in the Lord.
Live as children of light."

Day 227

Comparison will **snatch** your smile, **rob** your joy, and
hide you from the blessings God has **reserved** for you;
All because you are **comparing** yourself to them, **instead**
of you **focusing** on you.

Galatians 6:4
"Each one **should** test their own actions. Then they can take **pride** in
themselves alone, without comparing themselves to someone else."

Day 228

Joy **truly** is found **within.**
You can have all the friends, the **money,**
the latest **brands,** and the **perfect** GPA
and still not be **content with** who
and **how** God **created** you.
When you **discover** the joy that is within,
you will **never** miss out on the **peace** and **freedom**
God has **already** given to you.

Galatians 5:22
"But the **fruit** of the **Spirit** is love, joy, peace, forbearance,
kindness, goodness, faithfulness."

Day 229

It's **crazy** how we can **fall** more in love
with the **created** thing than with the **creator.**
When God is the **author** and **finisher** of our
entire existence.

Deuteronomy 6:5
"**Love** the Lord your God with **all your heart** and with all **your soul**
and with **all your strength.**"

Day 230

I **pray** for you.
I pray that God **brings** back your **creativity**
and your ability to **endure** the storm
while **showering** in the **sunlight** of God's Glory.
I pray that you **no longer** worry
because you **recognize** that God
never stops **supplying** your needs
and that the **only** thing you **have** to do
is **continue** to believe.

Hebrews 10:23
"Let us hold **unswervingly** to the **hope** we profess,
for He who **promised** is faithful."

Day 231

One of the **enemy's** tactics is to have us **fall** into sin
by **attacking** our **identity** and **tricking** us into **believing**
that God doesn't **love** us as much as He says He does;
but, sweet honey pie, **nothing** beats the enemy's lies
more than **standing firm** on your **faith**
with **integrity** and **pride.**

Isaiah 26:4
"Trust in the Lord **forever**, for the Lord, the Lord Himself,
is the **Rock** eternal."

Day 232

There is **healing,**
There is **peace,**
There is **love,**
beyond moments of defeat.
There is **sunshine** after storms and **restoration** during
wrong turns.
There is **strength** after **weakness** and **wholeness** when
you have **broken** into **pieces,**
all because of your **faith** in Jesus.

1 Peter 5:10
"And the God of all **grace,** who called you to His **eternal** glory in
Christ, after you have **suffered** a little while, will Himself **restore** you
and make you **strong**, **firm,** and **steadfast**."

Day 233

Sometimes it's not the **enemy** that's **stopping** me,
but sometimes it's **my inner me** that **intervenes**
with me being what God **created** me to be.

Romans 7:15
"I do not **understand** what I do. For what I want to do,
I do not do, but what I hate, I do."

Day 234

We **tend** to forget that **our** will
isn't **sufficient** enough to get us out
of the **situations** we **placed** ourselves in;
but it is by God's **favor**, **grace**, and **strength** that we are
forgiven for our sins and **placed** back in
position to **fulfill** God's mission.

2 Corinthians 9:8
"And God is able to bless you **abundantly**,
so that in all **things** at all times, having all that you need,
you will **abound** in every good work."

Day 235

What **scares** most people are the **unknowns** in life,
but what **keeps** one **grounded**
are the **promises** God has for His people.
So, when you're **feeling** unstable,
remember to **operate** not on your will, but on God's
because He'll **renew** your **strength** like a **soaring** eagle.

Isaiah 40:31
"…but those who hope in the Lord will **renew their strength.**
They **will soar** on **wings** like eagles; they will run
and not grow weary; they will walk and not be faint."

Day 236

Patience is one of the **fruits** of the spirit.
Its **seeds** grow into **leaves** that can help **avoid** misery
and **unnecessary** anxiety.
Don't rush, hush and let God's **timing** be your **priority.**

1 John 2:17
"The **world** and its **desires** pass away,
but whoever does the **will** of God **lives forever.**"

Day 237

How does one **find themselves** in the gospel?
By **seeing** themselves in each verse,
by **allowing** God to **speak** to the **heart** and not the **eyes,**
by **knowing** the word for **yourself**
and not by **prophetic** lies,
by **opening** up to God and **sharing** all the **emotions**
you've **experienced** on the **inside.**

Ephesians 6:17
"Take the helmet of **salvation** and the **sword of the Spirit**, which is
the **word of God**"

Day 238

When you fully **commit** yourself to God,
your **heart** and your **mind** will **begin** to **change**
as if you just **shaved** the parts of you that somehow
collided with who you truly are called to be.
When you fully **commit** yourself to God,
you become **free** from the parts of you that you **always**
wanted to leave.

Ephesians 4:23
"...to be **made** new in the **attitude** of your minds."

Day 239

Tomorrow is **never** promised.
Today isn't **forever**
and right now, is **never** too late.
Life is too **short** to **spread hate**
and too **beautiful** to not be great.
Never **forget** who created you
and always **remember** that every **minute** is a new
opportunity to make the **best** out of what
you choose to do.

2 Samuel 7:21
"For the sake of Your **word** and **according** to Your will, You have
done this **great** thing and **made** it **known** to Your servant."

Day 240

Endings are always **married** to sendings.
When **one** door closes,
another door is **cropped** open by **blessings.**
In **every** situation,
grow and **learn** from the lesson.

Proverbs 4:11
"I **instruct** you in the way of **wisdom**
and lead you along straight paths."

Day 241

God wouldn't **die** for you to not **speak** to you.
God is **always** speaking to us,
but our flesh **floods** God's voice
with the **sea** of our desires.
This is why it's so **important** to **unplug** and **rewire,**
because taking a **break** from our **own** flesh
sets us back on **fire** for God's **wisdom.**

Matthew 7:24
"Therefore, everyone who **hears** these words of **mine** and puts them
into **practice** is like a **wise** man who **built** his **house** on the **rock.**"

Day 242

New **month**, new **mindset**.
New **week, new goals.**
New **day**, new **attitude.**
New **hour**, new **accomplishments.**
Never let anyone **kill** your **time**
when every **minute** was **designed** for you to **shine.**

Psalms 31:16
"Let Your face **shine** on Your servant; **save me** in Your unfailing love."

Day 243

No need to **chase** after them
and **neglect** yourself of things you **enjoy** doing.
No need to fall into **depression**
by trying to **impress** someone that is **not worth** impressing.
You **deserve** to live and experience
heaven on earth.
Remember God has a **plan** for your life that
was given to you since birth.

Psalm 20:4
"May He give you the **desires** of your heart
and make all your plans **succeed**."

Day 244

Holy Spirit **fill** me up.
Remove my **fleshly** desires.
Remove any of my **weaknesses.**
Fill me up with Your **strength.**
Fill me up with **fire.**
Fill me up with **wisdom.**
Fill me up so I can **experience** freedom.

Psalm 107:9
"for He **satisfies** the **thirsty** and **fills** the **hungry** with good things."

Day 245

God is **perfect;**
God is **faithful;**
God is a God that **keeps** promises;
God is **patient;**
and God is **kind.**

Psalm 92:15
"...proclaiming, "The Lord is **upright**; He is my **Rock**,
and there is no wickedness in Him.""

Day 246

It's **heartwarming** to **reflect** on your life
and see how God's **hands** and **footprints**
are all over the **lines** of **your** story,
the **least** of what we can do is give God Glory.

1 Corinthians 10:31
"So, whether you **eat** or **drink** or whatever you do,
do it all for the glory of God."

Day 247

I **remember** the **days** when I couldn't **see** clearly.
I **remember** the **nights** when it felt like
God couldn't **hear** me,
but the **moment** that God **saved** me,
my **vision** became **focused**
and my **heart** and my **eyes** were **renewed** and **opened**.

Matthew 6:22
"The **eye** is the **lamp** of the body. If your **eyes** are **healthy**,
your **whole body** will be **full** of **light**."

Day 248

I still **feel** Your **presence** even when
I'm not **spiritually** present.
Your **presence** truly is a **present.**
A **gift** that is the **greatest** blessing.

Exodus 33:14
"The Lord replied, "My **presence** will go with you,
and I will **give** you **rest**."

Day 249

You keep me **grounded;**
You keep me **sound;**
You make me **happy,**
when I'm feeling **down,**
You make me **whole**
and You helped me **heal.**
God You're the **reason** I even **kneel** at nights
when life **gets** real.

Psalm 28:7
"The Lord is my **strength** and my **shield**; my heart **trusts** in Him,
and He helps me. My heart **leaps** for **joy,**
and with my song I **praise** Him."

Day 250

I want a **relationship** that **serves** God,
a relationship that **doesn't** make me **question**
what **side** my partner **truly** is on.
A relationship that has God's **touch,**
a relationship such as **Christ** and the **church.**

Ephesians 5:25
"Husbands, love your wives, just as **Christ loved** the church
and gave Himself up for her."

Day 251

It's better to **wait** and not **settle**
then to **settle** and then **later** wait.
Don't **rush** into something because you **feel** like God's
timing is too late.

James 1:12
"**Blessed** is the man who remains **steadfas**t under trial, for when he
has **stood** the **test,** he will receive the **crown** of life, which God has
promised to those who love Him."

Day 252

Trust the **process;**
Trust the **timing;**
Trust your **instincts;**
Trust the **red flags.**
Trust God
and I bet you'll **live** the **life** you **deserve** to have.

Psalm 33:20
"We **wait** in **hope** for the Lord; He is our **help** and our **shield**."

Day 253

So many **distractions** in this world;
So many **fake** people,
So many **haters,**
So many **followers,**
and not many **true** leaders,
which is **why** you
should **always** show up in the **world** as yourself
and not try to **pretend** to be somebody else.

Proverbs 17:22
"A **cheerful heart** is good medicine,
but a **crushed spirit** dries up the bones."

Day 254

I no **longer** want to **live** my **own** life.
I **surrender** my life to **Christ.**
God, I **desire** what You **desire** for me.
Let me **hear** You **loud** like the **waves.**
Let me see You **clear** each day.

Luke 11:28
He replied, "**Blessed** rather are those who **hear**
the word of God and obey it."

Day 255

God I just want to **make** You **proud** of me.
I just **want** to **please** You.
You have **done** so much for me that
there is **no** way I can **repay** You;
So, God **here** is my life,
I owe it all to You.

Romans 12:1
"Therefore, I urge you, brothers and sisters, in view of God's mercy, to
offer your bodies as a living sacrifice, holy and pleasing to God—
this is your **true and proper** worship."

Day 256

There's no **lips** soft enough to **sin** against You;
No **words** sweet **enough** to **disobey** You;
No **hands** warm **enough** to not **follow** You;
God, I **surrender** to You.

Luke 9:23
"And He said to all, "If anyone would **come after Me,** let him **deny himself** and **take up his cross daily** and **follow Me.**"

Day 257

This walk with God is **not** easy.
In this walk, you'll learn how to **trust,**
you'll learn how to **kill** your **own** desires,
you'll learn how to **talk,**
you'll learn how to be **patient,**
but most **importantly,**
you'll learn how to become **more** like Christ.

Proverbs 1:5
"Let the **wise listen** and **add to their learning,**
and let the **discerning** get guidance."

Day 258

When God tells you to **separate**
from **someone** you care about,
it feels like a **stab** in your **chest;**
but, when you're **walking** with God,
you have to **trust** that God
knows best.

James 1:22
"Do not **merely listen** to the **word**, and so deceive yourselves.
Do what it says."

Day 259

God, I **need** You daily
because life on my **own** will is **hard.**
I can't do this on my **own.**
Please let **tomorrow** be **better.**
Allow me to **control** my **thoughts**, my **temptations**, and
my **ungodly** desires.
God, I ask that tonight You **hold** my hand
and **relax** my **mind** like what **water** does to **fire.**

John 16:33
"I have told you these things, so that in Me you **may** have **peace.**
In this world you will have trouble.
But take heart! **I have overcome the world.**"

Day 260

God, I ask that You **redirect** my **focus** and as we walk side by side
I ask that the **song** the birds sing doesn't **drown** out Your voice,
or that the grass that **appears** green
doesn't rule out the choice
of daily **choosing** to follow You.

Psalm 1:3
"That person is like a **tree planted by streams of water,** which yields
its fruit in season and whose **leaf** does not **wither**—whatever
they do prospers."

Day 261

Father, You have **shown** me that
Your **presence** is **precious and**
Your **love** overcomes **lust.**
Your **grace** is **gentle,** and Your **words** are **forever** true.
God, I do not **want** to **live** a life that doesn't **include** You.

1 John 4:16
"And so, we **know** and **rely** on the **love God has for us.** God is love.
Whoever **lives** in love lives in God, and God in them."

Day 262

God, I **invite** You to be a **lamp** to my **feet**
and a **light** to my path
because at the **end** of it all,
it is Your **will** that I **rathe**r want to have.

Proverbs 19:21
"Many are the **plans** in a person's heart, but it is the Lord's **purpose**
that prevails."

Day 263

I **love** how You're **always** around to **listen** when I speak.
You're **always** near to help me **find** answers to the
questions I seek.
You're always **patient** and **affectionate**
to love me through my **growth** and **development.**

Philippians 4:5
"Let Your **gentleness** be **evident** to all. The Lord is near."

Day 264

God, I know that **part** of Your **plans** is to **prosper** me,
to leave this **world** a little bit **better** than what I found it.
I know that there are some **curses** I am **called** to **break**
and **generational wealth** and **money** I need to make.
God, I pray that You **guide me** to the path of the **keys** to
the doors I need to **open,** but cannot yet see.

Psalm 143:10
"**Teach me** to do Your **will,** for You are my God; may Your **good**
Spirit lead me on level ground."

Day 265

Each day You **strengthen** me;
You **renew** my **mind;**
You **heal** my **wounds;**
You **free** my **thoughts;**
and **straighten** my walk.
Life with You **provides** me with the **peace** I **need**
to live life with **contentment** and **serenity.**

Psalm 138:3
"When I called, You **answered** me; You **greatly** emboldened me."

Day 266

I want to be more **intentional** with You God
as You **walk** with me.
I don't just want to **walk** in **silence,**
but I want us to **talk** as our feet take steps **toward**
the **same** direction.
I want to know **You** as well as You know **me.**
I want to be **able** to **read** Your mind
and **complete** Your sentences.
I want to have the **relationship** You **envision**
for **us** to have back in Genesis.

Philippians 3:10
"I want to know Christ—yes, to **know** the power of His **resurrection**
and **participation** in His sufferings, becoming like Him in His death."

Day 267

I don't know how I'm going to **achieve** my highest goal,
but I do know that my **vision** of **high**
and God's vision of high is not the **same.**
I'm thinking **rich,** God is thinking **wealth.**
I'm thinking **house,** God is thinking **mansion.**
I'm thinking here on **earth,** but God has **heaven** in mind.
God, You tell us **not** to **focus** on **earthly** things,
but on all things **above,**
and as I **continue** to strive for **kingdom,**
everything I do **here** on earth **comes** from **love,**
loving You with all my **heart** and with **all** of my mind.

Matthew 22:37
Jesus replied: "**Love** the Lord your God with **all** your **heart**
and with all your **soul** and with all your **mind.**"

Day 268

When you are **healed,** you **become** free
from the **hurt, trauma,** and **pain;**
and when you **walk** with God each day,
you will be **made** brand **new;**
nothing will **ever** be the **same.**

Psalm 30:2
"Lord, my God, I **called** to You for **help,** and You **healed** me."

Day 269

Forgiveness is part of the **healing** process.
It's not **always** the **easiest** thing to do,
but as you **grow deeper** in God,
you will see that God **works** on your **heart**
allowing you to feel **brand new.**

Ephesians 4:24
"…and to put on the **new** self, **created** to be like God in **true**
righteousness and **holiness.**"

Day 270

God, I need You **daily.**
I need Your **strength;**
I need Your **will;**
and most **importantly** Your **guidance.**
In a world **full** of distractions,
I ask that You **guide** my **every** action,
help fill me up not only
with **grace** and **love**, but also with passion.

Matthew 6:11
"Give us **today** our **daily** bread."

Day 271

Many of us **neglect** the sabbath because
we **live** in a **culture** that
consistently wants to **grind, work,** and **chase** the "bag."
However, God **wants** us to have a **day to rest**,
a day where we can **relax** our **bodies**
and **mind** so that we can be **rejuvenated** to
fully fulfill our **assignment** in life.
Remind **yourself** that you are **not** alone.
God is by your **side** every **step** of the way, so don't be
afraid to say **not today.**

Hebrews 4:9-10
"There remains, then, a **Sabbath-rest** for the people of God; for
anyone who enters God's **rest** also **rests** from their works,
just as God did from His."

Day 272

You may not know all the **information,**
you may not have all the **answers,**
you may have never **seen** anyone in your **family**
achieve the goals God has **set** in your heart,
but you do have a **vision.**
You do have the **word** of God
and most **importantly** you have
the Holy Spirit **living** inside you;
therefore, there is NOTHING too **big** or too **small**
that God could not do.

1 Corinthians 1:9
"God is **faithful,** who has called you into **fellowship** with His Son,
Jesus Christ our Lord."

Day 273

You are the one.
You are the one that is going to **break curses.**
You are the one that is going to **lead**
your **family** to breakthrough.
You are the one that will **introduce**
God to the **next** generation.
It is you.
So, don't you dare **give up!**
Don't you dare get **caught** up in this **world's** distractions!
Stay **focused** and let God's **promises** guide your actions.

Proverbs 4:25
"Let your **eyes** look **straight** ahead; fix your **gaze** directly before you."

Day 274

There are going to be **moments**
when it **seems** like God is **silent** and you do not know
what God is **saying,**
but as I walk with God, I **came** to the **conclusion**
that during these **moments** you have to recall what God
had **already** told you.
This is the **foundation** of faith.

Psalm 62:6
"**Truly** He is my **rock** and my **salvation**; He is my **fortress;**
I **will not** be shaken."

Day 275

2020 is a year where **many** things **do not** make sense.
It is a year that **requires** you to show up
differently each day.
God likes to call us out of our **comfort** zone.
God is **fluid,**
God is not **confined to time**.
When He **calls** you or **pauses** your world
and **shifts** your routine,
it is because He is **preparing** you to grow,
so be ready to **receive** a new **blessing.**

Numbers 6:26
"The Lord turn His face **toward** you and give you **peace.**"

Day 276

God, I **need** You.
Every **day** I want to be in Your **presence;**
Every **meal** I want to give You **thanks;**
Every **night** I want to **talk** to You;
Every **second** I want to **serve** You.
The **peace** that You have **placed** in my **heart** during a
time of **chaos** speaks **volumes.**
Never in my **life** have I **ever** felt so much **joy**
just **being** on my **own.**
God, I thank You for **being** patient with me
and for **never** making me **feel** like I am alone.

Psalm 126:5
"Those who **sow** with **tears** will **reap** with **songs** of joy."

Day 277

You did not **wake up** this morning on **accident**
and you are not at your **final** destination.
God has a **vision** for your life.
God has **purpose** for your life.
And right now, your **future** through your lens, may be
blurry and you may be **weary,**
but my love, God is a God of **promises;**
however, the only way to **know** what
God has in store for you,
is for you to **build** your relationship
and **begin** walking with God.

Deuteronomy 31:6
"Be **strong** and **courageous**. Don't fear or be in dread of them,
for it is the Lord God who goes with you.
He will not **leave you or forsake you."**

Day 278

Lord I do not **always** know what I am **doing**,
but I **trust** that if I'm doing **something**
wrong, you will **correct** and **protect** me.

Proverbs 15:32
"Those who **disregard** discipline **despise** themselves, but the one who
heeds correction gains understanding."

Day 279

God, You know the **plans** You have for me.
Help me **destroy** the **timeline** I may have **created**
for **myself** that doesn't **align** with what You have **planned.**
Help me **stay** focused on the **bigger** picture,
because **whatever** You do not want for me
I do not want either.

Proverbs 16:1
"To **humans** belong the plans of the **heart,** but from the **Lord** comes
the **proper** answer of the tongue."

Day 280

Before every **decision** I make, Lord **help** me make it a
habit to speak to You first.
I want You to **lead me** and **guide** my every step.
Provide me with **wisdom** and **remove** any stress
because with You in my **heart,** I am **always** blessed.

Proverbs 16:3
"**Commit** to the Lord **whatever you do**,
and He will **establish** your plans."

Day 281

God **tonight** this poem isn't **written** for me.
Tonight, this poem is **written** specifically to **you**, the **one**
reading this poem.
Do **not give up** on **yourself**.
There is a God that has **already** fought
all of your **battles**.
The **victory** is already yours.

1 Corinthians 15:57
"But **thanks** be to God! He gives us the **victory**
through our **Lord Jesus Christ**."

Day 282

For the **bible** tells us that
God did not **give** us the **spirit** of **fear,**
but of **power, love,** and a **sound mind;**
therefore, **pray** more, **worry** less,
and **remember** that you are too
blessed to be **stressed.**

Psalm 119:143
"**Trouble** and **distress** have come upon me, but Your **commands**
give me **delight**."

Day 283

God **thank You** for **strengthening** me.
Thank You for **being** by my side.
Thank You for Your **patience** and Your **precious** time.

Psalm 9:1
"I will **give** thanks to You, Lord, with **all my heart**;
I will tell of all Your **wonderful deeds**."

Day 284

God, You know what You have in **store** for me.
You know what I **need.**
God **destroy** any **distraction**
that tries to **get in the way** of where **I am called** to be.

Isaiah 26:3
"You will keep in **perfect peace** those whose **minds are steadfast,**
because they **trust** in You."

Day 285

God will **wreck your** plans before **your plans** wreck you.
Never question who God **removes,**
trust God with **every** move.

Isaiah 55:8
"For **My** thoughts are not **your** thoughts, **neither** are **your** ways
My ways," declares the Lord."

Day 286

There is **power** in **not** allowing your **circumstances** to
overcome your peace because you **know** who's in **control.**
Being a **follower** of Christ **doesn't** mean an easy life,
being a **follower** of Christ means **peace** during **storms.**

Psalm 77:14
"You are the God who **performs** miracles; You **display**
Your **power** among the peoples."

Day 287

God **sees** what you **can't.**
Do not be **afraid** of **denial** and **rejection;**
because when God says **no,** it's for your **protection.**

Nahum 1:7
"The Lord is **good**, a **refuge** in times of trouble.
He **cares** for those who **trust** in Him."

Day 288

Do not go **seeking** purpose.
Seek the God that is the **author** of **purpose** and the
creator of your **existence**
and **through** your **pursuit** of God,
you'll meet **purpose** waiting for you at the **doorstep** of
your calling.

Proverbs 20:5
"The **purposes** of a person's **heart** are **deep** waters,
but one who has **insight** draws them out."

Day 289

Forgiveness is not the **same** as **acceptance.**
You can forgive someone for their **actions** while also
making it **clear** that their **actions**
are **unacceptable** and that as a **child** of God
you **deserve** to be **treated** better
and they **deserve** to **do** better.

Luke 17:3
So watch **yourselves**, "If your brother or sister sins **against** you,
rebuke them; and if they repent, **forgive** them."

Day 290

I am **always** so **amazed** at how You
can **transform** what was once **broken** back to being
brand new.
God, Your **love**, **grace**, and **mercy** shows that there's
nothing You **can't** do.
Lord, I **want** to **show** people that Your **existence** is real
and it's **true**.

2 Thessalonians 3:5
"May the Lord **direct** your **hearts** into God's **love**
and **Christ's** perseverance."

Day 291

God **knows** how **much** you **can** and **cannot** handle;
so, when life gets hard just know that God is **right**
in the rink **with you.**
When you feel like **throwing** in the towel,
He will **coach** you through **until** you make it through.

1 Corinthians 10:13
"He will not let you be **tempted** beyond what you can bear. But
when you are **tempted**, He will also provide a way out so that you
can **endure** it."

Day 292

Because God has **called** you to it, He will **help**
you get **through** it.
When you're going **through** a **transition** that feels
uncomfortable, it's so easy
to try to talk yourself **out** of what God
has talked you **into;**
but, **remember** that God is a **sovereign** God.
He **knows** you very well.
He **qualifies** the call even when
you already **disqualified** yourself
because you're **afraid** to fall.

1 Peter 2:9
"you may **declare** the **praises** of
Him who **called you out of darkness** into His **wonderful light.**"

Day 293

Today I find my **hands slipping** from Your **words.**
Today I find myself with my **mind cluttered**
by **uninvited** thoughts.
Thoughts of **failing;**
thoughts of **feeling** overwhelmed;
thoughts of **falling** behind the **best** version of myself.
God, **everyday** I am **reminded** of how
desperately I **need** Your help.

Psalm 71:2
"In Your **righteousness, rescue** me and **deliver** me;
turn Your **ear** to me and **save** me."

Day 294

Your **presence** is **peace** when there's **anxiety;**
Your **presence** is larger than **society.**
Your **presence** brings **healing** and **clarity;**
Your **presence** is **needed** for my **mentality.**

Philippians 4:4
"**Rejoice** in the **Lord** always. I will say it again: **Rejoice!**"

Day 295

My cup doesn't go a day **without** You **pouring** into it.
God even when I am **unworthy** of a refill
You **graciously** fill me up again.
God, let me be a **servant** to You and fill the **cups**
of **others** with Your grace
the **way** that You do.

John 4:14
"…but whoever **drinks** the water I give them will **never** thirst.
Indeed, the water I give them will **become** in them a spring of water
welling up to **eternal** life."

Day 296

Today was **rough.**
Today was **tiring.**
Today was **one** of those days
I felt like **giving up** on life, but I kept **reminding** myself
that it is only for a **moment**
and **moments** do not **define** our lives.
I kept **reminding** myself that
I will **make it** through today
because as long as I have **breath** in my **lungs,** I know that
God will **make sure** I'm okay.

Psalm 18:32
"It is God who **arms me** with **strength** and **keeps** my way **secure.**"

Day 297

When you find **yourself** stuck like sandals
in **deep** sand water,
remember the **promises,**
remember the **scriptures,**
remember **ALL** the times
God came for you like **water** pushing back up the sandals
you **thought** you had **lost** forever.

Psalm 63:7
"Because You have been my **help**, therefore in the **shadow** of
Your wings I will rejoice."

Day 298

Growth and **change** are business partners that **meet** in
the **middle** of the **road** in order
to **experience** transformation.
Transformation **cannot** exist if there is **no** movement.
You are **required** to put **one** foot in **front** of the other
to **experience** improvement.

2 Peter 1:5
"For this very **reason**, make every **effort** to add to your **faith**
goodness; and to goodness, knowledge."

Day 299

Lord, I am **stressed**
due to the **amount** of work I have to do,
but Lord I **trust** in You.
I **trust** that I will be **more** than ok at the **end** of the day
because You **always** come through.

Romans 8:39
"Neither height nor depth, nor **anything** else in all **creation**,
will be **able** to **separate** us **from** the love of God that is in
Christ Jesus our Lord."

Day 300

The enemy wants us **tired** in the flesh,
so that we can be **exhausted** in spirit,
but God I know that I will **prosper**
as long as You are in it.

Psalm 4:8
"In **peace** I will lie **down** and **sleep**, for You alone, Lord,
make me **dwell** in safety."

Day 301

I am **tired,** but I **will not** quit.
I am **nervous,** but I **will not** feed into my nerves.
I sometimes have **imposter syndrome,** but I will
remember who God says I am.
I am **fearfully and wonderfully** made
and that's the part that **keeps** me
grounded in who and whose I am.

Psalm 139:14
"I **praise You** because I am **fearfully and wonderfully** made;
Your works are **wonderful**, I know that full well."

Day 302

This **season** in my life **requires** me to stretch.
Stretch **long** and **far** like legs at the **end** of a
400-meter dash run.
Stretch like Jesus' **hands** on the cross.
God **never** said it would be **easy,**
He just **continues** to show us that it will be **worth** it.

2 Timothy 4:7
"I have **fought** the **good fight**, I have **finished** the race,
I have **kept the faith.**"

Day 303

When you **begin** to **understand** what is **attached** to you
not **falling** into sin,
not **giving up** on your **goals**, and not **entertaining** the
wrong people out of **boredom,**
then you **truly** begin to **live** like the **answer** to your
ancestor's prayers.
You'll feel **fired up** and **inspired** to **break** the chains of
generational curses.

Psalm 107:14
"He **brought them** out of **darkness**, the utter darkness,
and **broke away their chains.**"

Day 304

There are so **many** moments in our lives
where we are the **victim,**
but **in it** and **through it** all,
we are still the **victor.**

Deuteronomy 20:4
"For the Lord your God is the **one who goes with you to fight** for
you **against** your enemies to give you **victory**."

Day 305

When you **do not see** God's **hand** in it, just know that
God's **heart** is in it.
He is **working** when it **feels** like He is not, and He is
near when He feels like He is **far.**
God **knows** what you are **going through** and **trust** that
He knows **who** you are.
You **light up** in His **heart** like the **brightest star.**

Deuteronomy 11:12
"It is a **land** the Lord your God **cares for;** the **eyes** of the Lord your
God are **continually** on it from the **beginning** of the year to its end."

Day 306

God I **fear** not.
God I **worry** not.
Because Your **words** have **shown** me
that they **NEVER** stop **being** true;
so, no matter what **happens** in this world,
I know that You **WILL** always come through.

Psalm 34:4
"I **sought** the Lord, and He **answered** me;
He **delivered** me from all my fears."

Day 307

I know that You are **real** because when I **call** on you, I
instantly feel your **presence.**
A **warm** blanket feeling in a **chilly empty** room
reminding me that **You** are **always**
near and **powerful** enough to **shift** the atmosphere.

Genesis 1:3
"And God said, "Let **there** be **light**," and **there** was **light.**"

Day 308

When I began to seek the **totality** of God, our
conversations began to **sound** differently
and not only did my **mindset change,** but so did the
outfit of my **heart** and the **makeup** of my **stance.**
So much so that in **every** season whether **good** or **bad** I
am **able** to **endure** and **dance**
because I know that my God is a God
that is **good** in every **circumstance.**

1 Chronicles 16:34
"Give **thanks** to the Lord, for He is **good**; His love **endures** forever."

Day 309

Fill me up to the **point** my legs **elevate** off the ground
as if I became a solid color balloon **floating**
in the **bright** clear sky.
Fill me up to the point where my **existence**
catches someone's eye
wondering what I am **full** of
and when they take a **closer** look, they won't see me
but **all** of You.

Colossians 2:9
"For in Christ **all the fullness of the Deity** lives in bodily form."

Day 310

God help me **stay** focused.
Help me stay **free** from **distractions.**
Help me **become** the woman You **created** me to be.
Help me **achieve**, **succeed**, and **continue** to believe
when it **becomes** hard to see
all the **blessings** You have **already** given me.

James 1:17
"Every **good** and **perfect** gift is from above, coming down from
the Father of the heavenly lights, who **does not change**
like shifting shadows."

Day 311

It may be **pouring** today,
but there will be **sunshine** tomorrow.
It may be **cold** this minute, but you'll feel
the **warmth** from His love.
It may **look** dark now,
but there is **light** on the way.
I say all this to say **NEVER** give up on the Lord,
continue to seek him and pray.

Isaiah 40:29
"He gives **strength** to the weary and **increases** the power
of the weak."

Day 312

There's going to be **days** when you **realize** that you really
can't do life **without** God,
because **breakthroughs**
does not require your **might** or your **will,**
but the **Holy Spirit.**

Zechariah 4:6
"Not by **might nor by power,** but by My Spirit,'
says the Lord Almighty."

Day 313

Sometimes we need to **stop talking** to God
and **listen** to God.
God is **always** speaking,
it's just we are **not** always listening.

Jeremiah 33:3
"**Call** to Me and I **will** answer you and tell you **great** and
unsearchable things you do not know."

Day 314

The God I serve **always** exceeds **expectations,**
so I pray that we **hold** on to every **word**, every **promise**,
every **revelation**
no matter how many **twists** and **turns** we
encounter on our way to the **final** destination.

Romans 8:25
"But if we **hope** for what we do not yet **have**,
we **wait** for it **patiently**."

Day 315

God, today I pray for **discernment.**
Allow me to **decipher** your voice **verses** mine
until the time when Your **voice** and **mine** align.

1 Thessalonians 5:21
"but **test** them all; **hold on** to what is good."

Day 316

Today Lord, I will **hold** on to the **words** You **have already** spoken to me
and stop **searching** for a **new** word.
Lord, today I **ask** that You **remove** the **desires** of my **heart**
that has already **removed** You from **being** within it.
Lord, I ask that You **renew** my **spirit.**

Psalm 23:3
"He **refreshes** my soul. He **guides me** along the right **paths**
for His name's sake."

Day 317

You are **perfect** in **ALL** Your ways.
You **hold** onto **ALL** Your promises
even **during** times when the **promise** seems to have **died.**
Your **timing** is **perfect,** and You are God
through the **good**, the **ugly**, and the **rough** times.

Psalm 143:8
"Let the **morning** bring me word of Your **unfailing love**,
for I have put my **trust** in You."

Day 318

God is not **binded** by what **binds** you.
He is **almighty.**
He is **Lord.**
He is the **word**
and so, when God **speaks,** it is so! Whether He **roars** it
out **loud** or **whispers** very low,
His **yes** is His **yes**
and His **no** is His **no.**

Luke 1:37
"For **no** word from God will **ever** fail".

Day 319

I **don't** have **all** the **answers,** but **You** do.
I **don't** see **pass** the **corner,** but **You** do.
I **don't** hear the **conversations** behind my back,
but **You** do;
that is why I **always** and, in all ways, need to **trust** You.

Proverbs 29:25
"Fear of man will **prove** to be a **snare**,
but whoever **trusts** in the Lord is **kept safe.**"

Day 320

God works in **mysterious** ways
even **during** the days when it **feels** like He is **not** working.
This book was **birthed** through **your** vision.
I thank God for **creating** us in His **image.**
I thank God for our **collision,**
for our paths to have **collided.**
I can't thank God **enough** for **blessing** me with **a friend**
like **you** by my side.

Proverbs 27:9
"Perfume and incense bring **joy** to the **heart,** and the pleasantness of
a **friend** springs from their **heartfelt advice**."

Day 321

Gratitude **shifts** your attitude.
Therefore, **give** God **praise** on the **days** when
the sky is gray,
that's when you **experience** the God that makes a **way**
out of no way.

Hebrews 10:35
"So do not throw away your **confidence;** it will be **richly** rewarded."

Day 322

God, it is **Your** will over **mine.**
I don't want it, if you **haven't** blessed it.
Develop me to **become** more **guided** by the spirit
over being **guided** my **feelings.**

Galatians 4:6
"Because you are His sons, God **sent** the Spirit of His Son into our
hearts, the Spirit who calls out, *"Abba*, Father."

Day 323

God, You are **seated** high and yet You **look** low.
You know the **troubles** of our **hearts** and of our **mind**
and even **though** Your word tells us to not be anxious,
to not **fear**, to not **worry**,
and to not **lose** sight of Your **promises,**
we still **sometimes** do.
However, that **doesn't** stop You from making **new**
miracles in our lives
and **listening** to our cries.

Isaiah 40:8
"The grass **withers** and the **flowers** fall,
but the word of our God **endures forever**."

Day 324

Help me **become** more of **You** and less of **me**.
More of Your **spirit** and **less** of my **flesh.**
More of your **thoughts** and **less** of my **doubts.**
Fill me up in any **area** where there may be **droughts.**

Psalm 142:2
"I **pour** out before Him my **complaint**;
before Him I tell my **trouble**."

Day 325

God, Your **word** says that we can do **all** things
through You,
and when I **reflect** on my life, I **know** that to be true
because there is **no** way I am **able** to do **all**
the things I've **accomplished**
if it wasn't for You **being** a God
that **keeps every promise.**

Joshua 21:45
"Not one of all the Lord's **good promises** to Israel **failed**;
everyone was **fulfilled.**"

Day 326

God, today I **pray** that You **surround** me
with people that won't **lead** me to **stumble,**
but will **lead** me to have a **stronger walk** with You.
I **pray** that I come across people who are **spirit led** and
can be my **accountability** partners,
so, the days where I am **weak**
I'll have someone **translate** Your words when it's hard to
hear when You speak.

Proverbs 27:17
"As **iron** sharpens **iron**, so one person **sharpens** another."

Day 327

God, my **heart** is **full,** and my **mind** is at **peace.**
Walking with You puts **everything** to ease.
If there is **one** thing, I'm **grateful** for,
it is Your **grace** and **mercy.**
Thank You for walking with me and
showing me that I am **worthy.**

Proverbs 3:15
"She is more **precious** than **rubies,** nothing you **desire**
can **compare** with her."

Day 328

God, Your **word** says that
no **eyes** have **seen,**
no **ears** have **heard** the **plan** You have **set** for us,
which is why we should **never** be jealous of our **neighbor.**
God has a **new** miracle for you
beautifully wrapped with **your name engraved**
on the ribbon.
You just have to trust God **and** His vision.

Psalm 33:11
"But the **plans** of the Lord **stand** firm forever, the **purposes** of
His heart through all generations."

Day 329

There are **many** things that I am **grateful** for and one of
those **things** is having the **opportunity**
to **walk** with God.
I could've had taken a **different** path,
but this is the **journey** I prefer to have.

Deuteronomy 8:6
"**Observe** the **commands** of the Lord your God, walking in
obedience to Him and revering Him."

Day 330

God, You are so **good** to me.
I can feel Your **presence** everywhere I go,
a feeling of **safety** and **love**,
a feeling that **continues** to grow.

Psalm 63:3
"Because Your **love** is better than life, my lips will **glorify** You."

Day 331

There is no better **timing** than God's **timing.**
No better **plan** than God's **plan.**
No better **love** than God's **love.**
He is the **Great I Am.**
Therefore, with Him is **where** I stand.
With Him I **can** do **all** things **through** Him who
strengthens me.

Psalm 86:5
"You, Lord, are **forgiving** and **good**, abounding in **love**
to all who call to You."

Day 332

God **continue** to **speak** to me,
allow me to know **everything** I **need** to know to **draw**
closer to **Your** plan.
I know that I **can't** do it **all**, but You **definitely** can.

Psalm 36:5
"Your **love**, Lord, **reaches to the heavens**,
Your **faithfulness** to the skies."

Day 333

I think about my **future** often and the **desires**
I have in my **heart.**
I know that God is **good** and **everything** will piece
together the way that it should be.
I just have to **sit** back and **trust** that God
will do what He said He would.

Psalm 13:5
"But I **trust** in Your **unfailing love**;
my heart rejoices in your **salvation**."

Day 334

The **key** is to **not** worry,
but to **meditate** on God's **promises**
and **remember** you're **worthy**.
You may **not** be where you **want** to be,
but you're **definitely** not where you **used** to be and that in
itself is the **beauty** of God's mercy.

John 14:1
"Do not let your **hearts** be **troubled**. You **believe** in God;
believe also in Me."

Day 335

Life is **full** of **surprises.**
You **never** really know what God has up His sleeves,
but whatever it is, best **believe** that **most** times it's not always
what you **want,** but what you **need.**

Psalm 90:14
"Satisfy us in the **morning** with Your **unfailing love**, that we may
sing for **joy** and be **glad** all our days."

Day 336

The **lies** and the **secrets** that we **tell** and we **keep**,
will have you **sleep** on the **you** God **created** you to **be**.
Free **yourself** from that **bondage** and **walk** in truth
knowing that you are not perfect,
but at least you are **living** in **truth.**

2 Corinthians 3:17
"Now the Lord is the **Spirit**, and where the **Spirit of the Lord** is,
there is **freedom**."

Day 337

My biggest **challenge** on this walk is having **discernment**.
I've **learned** that a **good** opportunity with **bad** timing,
is a **curse**
and a **good** opportunity with **good** timing, is a **blessing**.
Being able to **decipher** your timing from God's
is a **great** lesson.

Proverbs 1:7
"The **fear of the Lord** is the **beginning** of **knowledge**, but fools
despise wisdom and instruction."

Day 338

This time **last year** I was a **broken** masterpiece
not yet **knowing** I was on the **verge** of
breaking completely.
A year later, I **witnessed** God **piece** all
my **pieces together**
making me **whole** again,
no longer **leaking,**
no longer **bleeding.**
I am healed
and that's a **wonderful** feeling.

Psalm 34:5
"Those who **look to Him** are **radiant**; their faces
are **never** covered with **shame.**"

Day 339

The minute Peter **took his eyes off** Jesus,
he **began** to sink.
He became **distracted** by his **environment.**
Lord, **help me** to not be **distracted** by this world,
but to be in **constant motivation** to keeping
my eyes on You
because **once** I'm **set** on You
there is nothing I can't do.
You make **all things possible** and **all things new.**

Hebrews 12:2
"Fixing our eyes on Jesus, the **pioneer and perfecter of faith**."

Day 340

The **wrong** relationship
will **sail** you out **far away** from your purpose.
It will **step** you **outside** of God's will.
It will distort your **vision,** your **aspirations**,
and your **dreams.**
It will **rob** you of your **peace** and **kill** your **joy.**
This is why it's **important** to pray **before** you get your
heart involved with **another** soul.
Ask God for **confirmation** then **wait**
and see if He says **Go.**

Psalm 37:7
"Be **still** before the Lord and **wait patiently** for Him."

Day 341

There are some **decisions** you **need** to make that
you have been **telling** yourself you are **waiting** on God,
but in **reality,** God is **waiting** on you.
He has **already** spoken, now it's **your time** to do what
you've been **told** to do.

John 14:15
"If you love Me, **keep My commands**."

Day 342

When God **tells** you to do **something** do not let the
massiveness of the **task**
make you **fall** into **disobedience.**
When God **speaks,** He **speaks** with **authority** and
already knows what you're **going** to **experience.**
When He **said** let **there** be light, **there** was light;
and still to **this day**, there **is** light.
Remember to trust the process and walk by **faith** and **not**
by **sight.**

1 Corinthians 2:5
"So that your faith **might not** rest on human **wisdom**,
but on God's **power.**"

Day 343

Letting go is hard, but **holding** on to what God
wants you to **release** gets in the way of you **receiving** your
blessing and **living** in peace.
Trust that what God **has** in **store** for you
is **better than** what you're **holding** on to.

Isaiah 43:1
"**Forget the former things**; do not **dwell** on the past."

Day 344

I **met** peace when I **met** God and **from** our **first**
encounter my life
has **never** been the **same.**
God **allow me** to experience
You in **a new** way, **each** and **every day.**

Colossians 3:15
"Let the **peace** of Christ **rule** in your hearts, since as **members** of **one**
body you were **called** to peace. and be **thankful.**"

Day 345

Holy Spirit dwell in me,
make **Yourself** at home.
For I had **cleaned up** the mess from the **brokenness** left
behind from my **scars.**
Not by my **strength,** but by **Yours** because You **never**
truly left me.
You were at the **corner** of every **single** door.

Isaiah 11:2
"The **Spirit of the Lord will rest on him**— the Spirit of **wisdom and
of understanding**, the Spirit **counsel and of might**, the Spirit of the
knowledge and fear of the Lord."

Day 346

A **year** ago, I didn't **know** Jesus.
I was **living** life **self-righteously,**
guided by **my** own **flesh** and **my** own **desires,**
a place in which I was **headed** to **disaster.**
I am just **grateful** that I get to experience
the **before** and **after.**

Psalm 35:18
"I will give You **thanks** in the great **assembly**;
among the throngs **I will praise You**."

Day 347

God you keep **no good** thing **from** us.
If we **do not have** what we **believe** we **deserve**, it's
because You know when it is the **right time**
for us to **receive** that **blessing.**
Your **timing** is **perfect,**
Your **plan** is **flawless,**
Your **vision** for our lives is **idiosyncratic,**
which is why I won't **frown** or **panic**
about what **I** desire.
You are **a promise keeper**
and the best provider.

Psalm 84:11
"For the Lord God is a **sun** and **shield**; the Lord **bestows** favor
and honor; **no good thing does He withhold**
from those whose walk is **blameless.**"

Day 348

Fear and **faith** can **never** be roommates.
One **needs** to leave, while the **other** makes itself at home.
Let alone,
fear is **inevitable** and it is a **human** response.
What you do with **fear** corresponds with how you **flex**
your faith.

Hebrews 11:6
"And **without** faith it is **impossible** to please God, because **anyone**
who comes to Him **must believe** that He **exists** and that He **rewards**
those who **earnestly** seek Him."

Day 349

God, **purify** me.
Refine me.
Renew me.
Return me back to the **original** image
You had in **mind** when You **first created me.**
You are the only **validation** and **approval** I need;
so, if You are **not pleased,** then God **purify** me.

2 Corinthians 4:16
"Therefore, we do not **lose** heart. Though **outwardly** we are wasting
away, yet **inwardly** we are being **renewed** day by day."

Day 350

Do not let **social media**
dismantle the **person** you are **supposed** to be
all because you're **displaying** a **false** person
that you **post** to be.

Galatians 1:10
"Am I now trying to win the **approval of human beings**, or of
God? Or am I **trying to please people**? If I were still trying to please
people, I **would not** be a **servant** of Christ."

Day 351

Unaddressed pain and trauma doesn't **vanish** when you
find a partner.
God should be the **only** relationship
you **enter** into broken.
Because **no one** on **earth** can measure to the God, who
puts **ALL** things **together**
for **His** good.

Isaiah 38:17
"**In Your love** You **kept me** from the pit of **destruction;**"

Day 352

What has been **something** God **told** you, but you haven't
yet **followed** His instructions?
Being **disobedient** doesn't get you to your **blessing,**
instead it **keeps** you from it.

Matthew 7:24
"Therefore, everyone who **hears** these words of **Mine** and **puts** them
into **practice** is like a wise man who **built** his house on the **rock**."

Day 353

We tend to be **drawn** to what's **familiar**
and **everything** that feels familiar **isn't always** healthy.
That is why you **should** be **led** by the **Holy Spirit** and
not by the **flesh.**
You **could** be **drawn** to your **dysfunction**
instead to the **best** of what God **has for you.**

Isaiah 48:17
This is what the Lord says—your Redeemer, the Holy One of Israel:
"I am the Lord your God, who **teaches you** what is **best** for you, who
directs you in the way you should go."

Day 354

The way we **transform** is through
the **renewing** of our mind.
The **story** you **choose** to believe is **either** going to
advance you in life
or **leave** you **falling** behind.

Psalm 139:24
"See if there is any **offensive** way in me,
and **lead me** in the **way** everlasting."

Day 355

If there's **anything** I've **learned** from this year,
it is the **significance**
of being in a **relationship** with God.
In a year, where the **world** experienced the most chaos,
I've experienced the most **peace** due to
an **increase** of **prayer** and **faith**
and a **decrease** in **anxiety** and **fear,**
all because I **kept** God **near.**

Romans 8:6
"The mind **governed** by the **flesh** is **death,**
but the mind **governed** by the **Spirit** is **life** and **peace.**"

Day 356

Your **love** is the **love** that **keeps** on **getting** better.
God, **You are so good** always, even when I **don't deserve**
Your **grace** and **mercy**.
You **show me** that I am **not my sin,** that there is
NOTHING that can **separate** us.
Every day and every second You're ready to make us
brand new again.

John 3:16
"For God so **loved** the world that He gave His **one and only Son**,
that whoever **believes** in Him shall not **perish** but have eternal life."

Day 357

It is **important** to know what **season** you're in.
Each **season** in your life **requires** you to **focus** on
something new.
Not being able to **acknowledge** your season
will **set you back** from your **breakthrough.**

Psalm 31:15
"My **times** are in Your hands; **deliver** me from the **hands** of my
enemies, from those who **pursue** me."

Day 358

God, **thank You** for wrapping Yourself in **flesh** and
experiencing birth.
God, **thank You** for Your presence **here** on **earth.**

Psalm 56:12
"I am under **vows to You**, my God; I will **present** my **thank
offerings** to You."

Day 359

As this year **comes** to an end,
I look **forward** to the beginning of a **new** chapter.
A new year to **grow deeper** in **love** with God.
Deeper in love with myself
and **deeper in love** with the **man** God **has for me**.

Ephesians 3:19
"And to know this **love** that **surpasses** knowledge—that you may be
filled to the **measure** of all the **fullness** of God."

Day 360

I will **wait** on You Lord.
I am **done** with **trying** to do **life** my own way.
I **pray**, that with **each** day, I will be **able**
to **hear** You **clearly,**
so that I know when I **should** step out on Your **word**
or **sit still** and **stay.**

Psalm 25:5
"**Guide me** in Your **truth** and **teach me**, for You are God **my Savior**,
and **my hope** is in You all day long."

Day 361

I know that I **can** do **all** things **through** Christ
which is why when my **flesh** is weak,
I **rely** on the **Holy Spirit** to help me **float** and not **sink.**

Acts 1:8
"But you will **receive power** when the **Holy Spirit** comes on you;
and you will be my **witnesses** in Jerusalem, and in all Judea and
Samaria, and to the ends of the earth."

Day 362

I'm so **grateful** for the **healing** process.
I'm so grateful for this **journey** to being **whole again.**
I hope to never find **myself** in a **relationship**
where I **end** up **losing** me.
Being in a **relationship** with the **wrong person**
not only **derails you from God**,
but **also** from **your destiny**.

Psalm 69:30
"I will **praise** God's name in **song** and glorify Him
with **thanksgiving**."

Day 363

I'm **excited** for all that **this new year** has in store.
When you're **walking** with God,
just **prepare** for all the **open doors**.

Romans 8:19
"For the creation **waits** in **eager** expectation for the **children**
of God to be revealed."

Day 364

God Your **word** says to **believe** and I will **receive**
whatever I **ask** for in **prayer.**
Lord, You and I **know** the things I have **asked** for and
things I **desire.**
I know that my **desires align** with **Yours.**
The **challenge** is to **trust** Your **timing** and not **mine,**
since You are a God that is **sovereign**
in **everything** even with **time.**

Psalm 115:3
"Our God is in **heaven**; He does **whatever** pleases Him."

Day 365

When I look at the **receipt** for all that God
has **done** for me,
there is no doubt that **He is faithful.**
There is no doubt that **He is good.**
There is no doubt that **He is working**
through **me** and **in me,**
and for that reason, it is my **duty** to **ensure** that He gets
ALL of the **glory.**

Psalm 3:3
"But You, Lord, are a **shield around me**, my **glory**, the One **who
lifts my head high.**"

Day 366

Healing isn't a **destination.**
Healing is a journey
and the **walk** with God c o n t i n u e s.........

Psalm 106:1
"**Praise** the Lord. Give **thanks** to the Lord, for **He is good**; His love
endures forever."

Thank You

BLAMELESS

Made in the USA
Middletown, DE
16 July 2021